Quit Smoking
with the
Nicotine Phaseout Programme

Swift Publishers, England.
A subsidiary of Swift Consolidated Holdings PLC

British Library Cataloguing-in-Publication Data

Steele, Chris
Quit Smoking
with the Nicotine Phaseout Programme
I. World — Medical Self Help
II. Title

ISBN 1 874082 02 2
© 1993 by Chris Steele

First published in Great Britain
by Swift Publishers 1993

Cartoons drawn by John Williamson

Typeset by Armitage Typo/Graphics, Riverside Studios
Dogley Mill, Fenay Bridge, Huddersfield HD8 0LE

Printed and bound in the UK by Harper Collins.
Wester Hill Road, Bishopbriggs, Glasgow G20

Quit Smoking with the Nicotine Phaseout Programme

Dr Chris Steele

SWIFT
PUBLISHERS

Swift Publishers
Refuge Assurance House, Market Street,
Bromsgrove, Worcestershire, B61 8DA England.

Contents

For Monica, Anne-Marie, Matthew, Catherine and Andrew, my mother and Jack.

Acknowledgements

I would like to thank the first two smokers I ever treated, way back in 1978 – Benny van den Burgh and Maxton G. Beasley. They were both friends who bravely volunteered to help me in my initial research. The treatment they went through was quite horrific, involving the aversion therapy you will find described in the introduction. I know what they experienced, as Benny kindly offered to put me through this unmitigated torture too. Thanks Benny! I felt so ill, I just wanted to die. Thankfully, our friendship survived. How wonderful that we can offer smokers a much gentler way of quitting these days.

I would like to take this opportunity of thanking the thousands of smokers who have attended my Stop Smoking clinics over the past 15 years. What I have learnt from you, as you suffered the pangs of tobacco withdrawal, has been priceless and unique. You gave me a true understanding of the severity of nicotine addiction. Without your suffering, this book would not have been possible.

I would also like to thank Dr Frank Ryan, author of the highly successful *The Eskimo Diet*, for his patience and advice in reading the typescript. Frank and Swift Publishers have been very helpful and tolerant.

Finally a big thank-you to John Williamson, the cartoonist, for the delightful drawings which so cleverly and humourously interpret the salient points of the text. I hope you, the reader, can smile quietly at his understanding of what you are going through in quitting smoking!

Introduction

By Dr Frank Ryan, co-author of *The Eskimo Diet*

If you are a smoker, this book is likely to be one of the best presents you have ever bought or received. Follow the instructions carefully and you could change the course of your life. This might seem an exaggeration: but think what is at stake. You will be healthier, richer and, believe it or not, more confident – because you will have overcome an addiction that has been threatening both your life and your bank balance.

But don't be talked into trying anything yet. Chris invites you to sit yourself down, light a cigarette, and just give him time enough to convince you that you really can give up the smoking habit once and for all. Yes, you did read that correctly – **light yourself a cigarette, sit back, relax** ... and learn a little about Chris and his methods.

You may recognise Dr Chris Steele as the friendly and helpful doctor on the *This Morning* television programme. But Dr Steele is also widely recognised as an international expert on helping people to stop smoking. He has lectured and demonstrated his skills in more than 20 countries and as far afield as China, Japan and Australia.

He has personally trained an astonishing 6,000 British doctors in the art of helping people to stop smoking and he is in great demand as a public speaker because of his unrivalled experience in the field of 'Smoking Cessation'. Dr Chris Steele sees himself very much as the smoker's friend. It all began some 15 years ago when one of his patients came to see him and asked for help.

> "Doctor, as you know I've recently had a heart attack and the cardiologist has told me I must give up smoking. I've tried and tried but I just can't give up cigarettes for more than a couple of days. Is there anything you can do to help me?"

Chris felt very frustrated when he found there was nothing at all he could do to help. At that time there were few experts he himself could turn to for advice. It was quite a challenge and so he decided to learn more about it for himself. He began by looking very closely at what treatments were available. Everybody was well aware that smoking was more than a habit: it was an addiction. But Chris soon discovered that very little was being done to help smokers overcome their addiction to tobacco. Most of his medical colleagues, though well aware that smoking was causing a lot of illness, were simply telling their patients to give up smoking without offering any practical help. Smokers were expected to stop because the doctor had told them to do so. Failure was all too inevitable for many people, who suffered severe and troublesome withdrawal effects when they tried to stop.

It was obvious to Chris Steele that smokers needed a friendly expert, so he took up this challenge to become a pioneer in smoking cessation therapy. He now runs two NHS 'Stop Smoking' clinics in Manchester, one at the University Hospital of South Manchester, and the other at Wythenshawe Hospital, where the North-West Lung Centre and Regional Heart Transplant Centre are located. His clinics are the busiest in Europe and are very popular with smokers because he really does understand the problems of stopping smoking and has helped many thousands to quit over many years. He never wags his fingers at people but prefers to use humour and a light-hearted approach, so people enjoy their evenings on his 'Stop Smoking' courses. He personally helps up to 120 smokers at each session.

Over 15 years, Chris Steele has evolved his very own 'SMOKER'S TEN POINT QUIT PLAN'. This has featured in a three-part television programme for ITV. He has also founded 'SmokeQuitters' which provides stop-smoking courses for industry, where more and more employers are showing a keen interest in allowing their employees time off work to attend his 'Smoking Cessation' courses. Several years ago, British Telecom asked him to provide a 'Stop-Smoking' line service, which became the very successful 'SMOKER'S QUITLINE'. He even took the Government to task, compelling the Department of Health to make nicotine-containing gum available on prescription. Although it was a short-lived victory, smokers knew they had a champion who would fight for their cause even at the highest levels.

It will be obvious that Dr Chris Steele knows a great deal about helping smokers to quit. The corner-stone of this very successful new strategy is his acclaimed 'NICOTINE PHASEOUT PROGRAMME', which helps smokers to quit the habit with the minimum of withdrawal symptoms and, in this way, they are given a wonderful opportunity to stay tobacco-free for good. Anybody who knows smokers and their problems will realise what an achievement this really is. Chris is one of the most successful in the world because he understands the human difficulties involved. He delivers no sermons about the demon weed and makes no outrageous promises of success. He refuses to counsel reluctant quitters, preferring instead to help only those who are really determined to quit.

When he first began to study ways of stopping smoking, Chris had an open mind to all the new therapies that were being proposed. An attic in his home became his 'treatment room', where his patients would volunteer to try every possible treatment. He tried hypnosis and acupuncture, only to conclude they were not the answer. On another occasion, when he was trying out the newly recommended 'aversion therapy', a method designed to turn smokers against cigarettes, he scattered more than 2,000 soggy and mouldy cigarette ends over the treatment room floor. Smokers had to chain-smoke cigarettes in rapid succession until the combination of smoking and the atmosphere of stale cigarette ends caused them to vomit. What an unpleasant treatment! Chris supported his patients through the ordeal − an ordeal every bit as unpleasant for this caring doctor as for his desperate patients. When the patients had recovered from their oversmoking, they were further subjected to electric shocks while smoking some more cigarettes. The theory is obvious. No longer would smoking prove an enjoyable experience; the very thought of a cigarette would arouse feelings of nausea and pain. Well, so the theory went.

But in time it was obvious to Chris that the answer did not lie in anything so unpleasant. He was convinced that sooner or later a better option would come along, a method that was a good deal more friendly to people who genuinely wanted to stop smoking. And now, at last, he feels he has found this friendly method of helping people in his 'NICOTINE PHASEOUT PROGRAMME'. So what is this really about?

Firstly, it really is new. It is not a re-hash of all the old failed treatments. Indeed it is based on the most up-to-date scientific understanding of what makes people smoke and in particular of the real physical addiction to nicotine that lies at the heart of the craving. Dr Chris Steele's 'NICOTINE PHASEOUT PROGRAMME' is designed to wean the smoker away gradually and painlessly from that powerful addiction. Nor is it pie-in-the-sky based on the latest scientific fad or theory. His 'NICOTINE PHASEOUT PROGRAMME' has proved itself wonderfully successful for thousands of smokers, including many celebrities. For many smokers it has become the first successful means of escape from their addiction to tobacco.

As a hospital consultant of 22 years experience, and long involved in the battle against smoking-related diseases, I am convinced that in this book Chris Steele offers the smoker the best chance ever of giving up smoking and staying free for good.

Dr Frank Ryan

* * * * *

Chris Steele is married to Monica, an ex-nurse and midwife, and they have four children, Anne-Marie 21, Matthew 18, Catherine 14 and Andrew 8.

How to use this book

In order to become a successful ex-smoker, you must be strongly determined to give up your cigarettes.

You probably know that it is difficult to give up smoking because you have already tried several times and eventually gone back to your cigarettes. In fact, over 70 per cent of smokers have tried at least twice to quit smoking without success. Yet those who have become successful long term are people who were determined to keep 'having a go' at quitting before eventually 'making it'. There are about 10 million of these ex-smokers in the UK today, so you see it can be done, and *you can* do it!

With the 'NICOTINE PHASEOUT PROGRAMME' you have a very good chance of success, no matter that you have tried before and failed. This programme has already worked for thousands who are now grateful *long-term* ex-smokers.

Don't be afraid of trying to give up cigarettes. Many smokers who dreaded giving up were pleasantly surprised at how easy it proved to be – once they had put their mind to it. This book cannot stop you smoking. It can **help** you to stop but alone it cannot stop you. The decision to stop smoking is yours. The final crunch comes when you're dying for a smoke and someone offers you a cigarette. **YOU** must then decide whether you're going to smoke that cigarette or not. The easy solution is to take the cigarette and enjoy it, telling no-one you've had it. But you know that's not the right solution − you are only fooling yourself.

To be successful at quitting cigarettes you must feel strongly, deep down inside you, that you are going to do it. And, believe me, you can do it!

But first you must accept that there is no magic cure for the smoking problem. Your own determination and resolve along with this 'SMOKER'S TEN POINT QUIT PLAN' will help you to overcome the craving for cigarettes.

THE 'QUIT PLAN' IS COMPOSED OF THREE IMPORTANT STEPS:

1. Preparing to stop.

2. Stopping.

3. Staying stopped.

Each step is further divided into subsections to provide you with a comprehensive well proven 'Quit Plan'.

IT'S THE ONLY PLEASURE I GET
OUT OF LIFE.

The Smoker's Ten Point Quit Plan

The backbone of this 'TEN POINT QUIT PLAN' is **'THE NICOTINE PHASEOUT PROGRAMME'** – as featured in chapters 6 to 9 in this book.

To gain the best from this book, I would recommend that first you read Chapters 1 to 11, fairly quickly. Then come back to Chapter 1, and methodically work your way through the book again, deciding on your *Quit Day,* and then following the advice presented in the Quit Plan, as you read through the book for a second time. This advice is given so that you will from the very start have a basic understanding of how this Quit Plan is going to help you.

When you stop smoking you will be giving up your normal supply of nicotine – tobacco – and so, to make stopping smoking easier for you, I will be discussing some very new treatments which are usually called 'nicotine replacement therapies' but which I call 'nicotine phaseout therapies'.

These can be obtained from your own doctor or local pharmacist. Even if you have tried one of those treatments already, I would recommend that you try again, using the special techniques and extra 'tricks' that I have described in this book. So, before your second and more detailed reading of the entire book, you should have decided on which type of Nicotine Phaseout Therapy suits you and have that treatment ready to use, once you have given up your cigarettes.

It has been shown that smokers who use nicotine phaseout therapies double their chances of becoming successful ex-smokers. However, if you decide not to use any of these treatments, you can still proceed with the Quit Plan, by concentrating on the other items of advice which are, in themselves, effective methods of getting you through those early days of quitting cigarettes.

I wish you the best of luck in your efforts at giving up smoking. Just do your best and you might be pleasantly surprised. Many smokers who have used the Nicotine Phaseout Programme could not believe that stopping smoking could be so easy and pain-free.

After all, stopping smoking never killed anybody, whereas smoking kills more people every year in the UK than alcohol, heroin, cocaine, crack, suicide, murder, fires, car accidents and AIDS all put together.

So come on! Try hard! I really am going to help you, and *together*, I believe we can do it.

Section A

Preparing to Stop

Chapter 1

Quit Day!

CUTTING
DOWN ON
CIGARETTES

Many smokers will have already done their utmost to stop smoking. As very little expert guidance is available, they will have tried to quit using their own ideas or perhaps the ideas of well-meaning relatives or friends.

One popular method is to give up smoking gradually, by cutting down on the number of cigarettes smoked daily. This is aimed at helping you to quit in as painless a way as possible. On the face of it this idea seems quite reasonable since, after all, when you started smoking you did not suddenly start smoking 20 cigarettes a day. At first you only smoked perhaps one cigarette a day, then three, then five until eventually you became as it were stabilised on 20 cigarettes or more each day. Only gradually did you become a confirmed smoker.

So why not become a confirmed non-smoker gradually? Wouldn't you rather have two cigarettes a day than no cigarettes? And wouldn't a day with only five cigarettes be less severe on your nerves than a day without any cigarettes at all? Of course ... or so it would seem! But research has shown that smokers who attempt to give up smoking by this means are not generally successful in the long term.

CHANGING BRANDS

Changing to a milder brand in an attempt to wean yourself off cigarettes is not the ideal way to stop smoking either. In fact, smokers who change down to a milder brand will compensate by inhaling the smoke deeper, holding it in the lungs for longer, taking more puffs from each cigarette, smoking the cigarette closer to the filter or smoking more cigarettes per day. Their blood nicotine levels are more or less identical whether they are smoking their normal cigarettes or a milder brand.

SWAPPING TO CIGARS OR PIPE

When somebody who has recently given up smoking is sorely tempted to start smoking again, he will sometimes allow himself an occasional cigar, especially after an enjoyable meal or on a special social occasion. He is apt to tell himself that he doesn't smoke cigarettes, so he is allowed to enjoy that one cigar on extra-special occasions. And, of course, don't we all know what the eventual outcome will be ... the odd cigar on special occasions becomes a cigar every evening, and then three cigars a day and then five cigars a day, and so on. In the end this ex-cigarette smoker has now entered the more dangerous situation of smoking cigars regularly. Cigar and pipe smoke are far stronger than cigarette smoke and a cigarette smoker who changes over will inhale that stronger smoke into their lungs. This stronger smoke has much higher concentrations of tars and several other chemicals and so this smoke is more dangerous to the body.

It's rather interesting to note that those who have been lifelong cigar or pipe smokers don't inhale their smoke. In fact they don't need to inhale, because the smoke from cigar or pipe tobacco is alkaline and in an alkaline setting nicotine is readily absorbed into the bloodstream through the lining of the mouth. This nicotine is then transported to the brain where it exerts its pleasant effects. Watch how a pipe smoker just casually puffs on his pipe, without inhaling that smoke deep into the lungs.

On the other hand cigarette smokers inhale their smoke deep into the lungs to get their nicotine into the bloodstream. Cigarette smoke is the very opposite to cigar and pipe smoke: being acidic, the nicotine will not be absorbed across the lining of the mouth, where the medium is alkaline. However, the lining of the lungs will efficiently absorb all that inhaled nicotine when the smoke is deeply inhaled. So the deeply inhaled smoke of the habitual cigarette smoker readily delivers its nicotine into the bloodstream inside the lungs, after which it is transported to where it is craved – the brain.

Many cigarette smokers say they don't inhale but in fact they do. Most cigarette smokers are smoking to get nicotine into their bodies and the only way to achieve that with cigarettes is to inhale the smoke deeply. I have surprised many a smoker who denied inhaling by asking them to blow into a machine called a carbon monoxide monitor, which measures the level of gas in the bloodstream.

All smokers have carbon monoxide in their blood, some at very high levels. The gas gets there from cigarette smoke being inhaled into the lungs. So most cigarette smokers do inhale, some more than others; and if they stop smoking cigarettes and change over to cigars or pipe, they continue with their long-standing habit of inhaling, drawing this stronger and more dangerous smoke into their bloodstream. The message, therefore, is that if you must return to smoking, go back to your cigarettes and do not change to the stronger tobacco of cigars or pipes. You can always try again at a later date to give up cigarettes. So you see that cutting down, changing brands of cigarettes, or using cigars or a pipe are not methods I would recommend. If you really want to stop smoking, then the only way to do it is . . . to **STOP** smoking.

Now for some good news! When you stop smoking, your carbon monoxide levels drop so rapidly that within 24 hours the level of this harmful gas in your blood will be the same as a non-smoker, even though you may have smoked for 40 years. This is one of the very early and yet important benefits of stopping smoking. Quite a number of family doctors have these carbon monoxide monitors, so if you are seriously considering stopping smoking pop in to see your doctor and see if you can get your carbon monoxide measured before and after you stop smoking.

CHOOSING YOUR QUIT DAY

Come on now, when are you going to do it? When are **YOU** going to stop smoking? I want you to choose a day in the immediate future when you are going to give up your cigarettes completely. You will probably find all sorts of excuses not to stop on this day or that day, but to be honest there rarely is a perfect time to stop smoking. If possible, try to choose a time when you won't be under too much stress. Yet isn't it odd how stress just seems to rear its ugly head the moment you give up your cigarettes.

In my long experience, there is never a perfect time to give up smoking, so let's get into quitting as soon as possible.

You must commit yourself to naming the day on which you are going to stop smoking, by writing it down, so here goes!

MY QUIT DAY IS GOING TO BE

....

From that day on, I will be a non-smoker following the advice in this quit plan to achieve success!

Mark your Q-DAY on the Smoker's Quit Chart at the end of this book. Write a big 'Q' on the appropriate date. For each smoke-free day after 'Q' day, mark a tick on the chart – or, if you happen to smoke, mark that day with a cross followed by the number of cigarettes smoked.

QUITTERS' STORIES

Mr M.G.B., professional entertainer ...

"When I had tried to stop smoking before, I thought it would be far easier gradually to reduce the number of cigarettes I smoked each day. I was initially smoking 40 cigarettes per day and with great determination I set out upon my plan of campaign ... For the first week I reduced my cigarette consumption down to 30 a day, and that was no problem. The next week I went down to 20 a day, but I found myself panicking on the first day when I realised that I had only 15 cigarettes left to last me from 2.00pm to midnight.

"I kept telling myself that at least I was still allowed to smoke 20 a day, which was far better than having none at all. When I cut down to only 10 per day, the cravings were unbearable. As I was finishing one cigarette I was calculating how long I'd have to wait before I could have my next smoke. When I lit that next one it was sheer ecstacy ... but the cigarette seemed to last no time at all, and then I was craving badly for my next one.

"I was totally pre-occupied with thoughts of my next cigarette. My whole daily routine was centred on the timing of each cigarette and,

as I had planned to go from 10 a day to none, I dreaded the thought of having to live through a day without any cigarettes at all.

"In fact, I decided to ease the burden further by going down to 5 cigarettes a day rather than stopping, and as the day to stop approached I put off the dreaded day by reducing to 4 a day, then 3, 2 and finally 1 a day. I was only prolonging the agony and I'm telling you it was real agony. All through the days of gradually reducing I lived in fear of that ultimate 'day of execution' when I'd have to give up. I was spending abnormal amounts of time thinking of how enjoyable the next cigarette was going to be in exactly 49 minutes' time.

"Looking back to that attempt at quitting smoking, I now see that I was actually making it much harder for myself eventually to give up the habit; for I seemed to spend most of my time longing for the next cigarette and even making the smoking of that cigarette more and more enjoyable. I seemed to be reinforcing the enjoyment of my smoking rather than getting myself off the cigarettes.

"When I was told to 'name the day' and commit myself to stopping abruptly and completely on an agreed date

continued

in the immediate future, I panicked. That was not going to be easy to cope with, especially when I recalled the painful memories of gradually reducing my consumption of cigarettes.

"Anyhow I decided to follow the advice given, and although I faced the 'Quit Day' with trepidation it was much easier than I had anticipated. Naming the day was such a strong commitment that my resolve and determination seemed to be enhanced, and unlike when I was cutting down I felt positive rather than negative about the whole process of stopping smoking.

"It was far easier to stop suddenly than to taper down my cigarette consumption. I had never been successful at stopping smoking for more than two to three days before, but this time I was able to do it. By 'naming the day' I'd decided to stop at once, rid myself of cigarettes and get right into quitting immediately. It worked!

"My Quit Day was 15 years ago, and I haven't touched one since."

Chapter 2

Quit with a Friend

Once you've named your Quit Day you are free to begin setting up the support systems that will see you through the first difficult days and hopefully lay the foundation for a smoking-free future. Many of the people I have helped over the years talk about the great void that is created in their lives once they have stopped smoking. There seems to be an emptiness there, as if losing a friend. Many talk of loneliness — a feeling of being out on your own in a world full of people not only smoking but enjoying every minute of it as well.

By finding someone to join you in your resolve to give up cigarettes, you will avoid the loneliness and create for yourself an ally who will always know exactly what you are going through, as the pair of you work your way through this quit programme.

Try to persuade a friend, workmate or a member of your family to give up their cigarettes at the same time as you do — but make sure it's a person who genuinely wants to quit because determination is the only real key to success. Many people assure me that quitting with a friend helps ease the pain of withdrawal because it ensures that a problem shared is, indeed, a problem halved. In America this method of quitting with a friend is called the 'Buddy' system — find a buddy to quit with you. Seems like a 'buddy' good idea!

Let's look for a start at some of the danger areas for the person trying to kick the habit alone. Loneliness I've mentioned, and along with it comes a feeling of persecution. For those first few days it can appear that everyone is against you. Smokers don't want you to stop because, if you succeed, you will have shown yourself to have more willpower than them.

Let's face it, the majority of smokers would like to give up and many of them will have tried unsuccessfully to kick the habit at least once. These people will turn out to be your worst enemies when you are at your most vulnerable. Tell them you're trying to give up and they'll do everything in their power to persuade you to have a cigarette.

> "Go on, just the one", they implore you.
> "Look, you've been stopped for a week, so **one** cigarette is not going to harm you."

Don't be fooled: it's often that very one that starts you on the road back to 20 or 30 a day.

Beware also the former smoker. On the face of it he or she should be your friend and a source of encouragement but in the midst of withdrawal he or she can deal a cruel blow to your confidence with comments like:

> "Well I gave up without any problems at all and certainly didn't need any outside help."
> or . . .
> "Me, I just stopped smoking overnight, and I was on 40 a day for 30 years . . . I can't see what your problem is."

Wonderful morale-boosting stuff, but don't think that non-smokers are going to be a lot of help either because for a start they have never experienced what you are going through in the first days after quitting. They have never been hooked to the craving for a smoke; they have never felt that build-up of tension that panics the smoker who cannot get her or his hands on a cigarette. Only the smoker knows how quickly that tension or craving is relieved once a cigarette has been lit up and the smoke inhaled.

So if — in general — smokers, ex-smokers and non-smokers can't or won't help you, what can you do? You'll probably find your family supportive but you must ensure they don't underestimate the feelings you're experiencing, so sharing the problem with someone who's experiencing the same withdrawal symptoms makes a lot of sense. Find someone prepared to give up smoking on the same day as you and then follow these simple guidelines.

★ Arrange to ring each other at least once a day for the first couple of weeks to compare notes and check progress.

★ If possible, quit with a workmate so that you share withdrawal experiences with someone you spend a lot of time with — moral support is an important factor over the period immediately following Quit Day.

★ Pick up the phone the moment you feel a craving coming on and talk about it. Express yourself openly and freely and, more often than not, you will feel much better for it.

★ If you're married and your partner is also a smoker, try to persuade them to join you in your Quit Plan. In my experience a husband and wife giving up together make the strongest of all quit teams.

★ Draw up a friendly contract between you and your quit 'buddy', perhaps promising to pay them the money you will have saved from not smoking if you fall by the wayside and take up the habit again. I've included a sample contract at the end of this passage but the actual wording of the agreement is up to you. Quitters who have tried it say it's very useful as an extra incentive in times of great temptation.

THE QUIT CONTRACT

We

(i) ....

and

(ii) ....

agree to quit smoking on the following pre-arranged Quit Day:

....

The current price of a packet of cigarettes is

....

From the morning of our Quit Day we will both endeavour not to smoke at any time. Should one of us fail to keep off cigarettes for a period of

.... (enter 3, 6 or 12 months) then that person will pay the other a sum of money

equal to the cost of .... (enter 200, 500, or 1000) cigarettes.

Signed: (1) ....

(2) ....

Dated ....

QUITTERS' STORIES

Mrs. J. B., housewife . . .

"My husband and I decided to stop smoking together. On previous attempts I had tried to stop on my own and that was very difficult, for he would sit down after his evening meal, watch the television and have his cigarette with his cup of coffee. As that was our usual daily routine, it was extremely difficult for me just to sit there dying for a cigarette whilst he sat there with a smug smile on his face. I couldn't stand the temptation for long, and so I eventually succumbed and sneaked a few puffs from his lighted cigarette when he left the room to go to the toilet. This whetted my appetite for a smoke so much that I was back to smoking again within a couple of days.

"At that time he didn't want to give up his cigarettes and so life for me without my cigarettes was very trying indeed. This time I asked him to try and stop with me ... he agreed! It has made all the difference to my quitting progress, for I have been able to help my husband give up smoking and he has been very supportive of me in my attempt. We are therefore helping each other, and every evening we now compare our progress during the day.

"To suffer together is to ease the suffering. At least you know that you are not on your own, and you also feel very determined not to be the weaker partner by being the first to give in to a cigarette. So you just keep going ... and you stay off cigarettes!"

Mr. J.T., engineer ...

"I told three friends at work that I was thinking of stopping smoking. One had recently developed bad circulation in his leg and had been strongly advised by his doctor to stop smoking, so he was keen to stop. The other two just felt that they couldn't afford to continue smoking. So we all decided to stop smoking together on the following Monday morning.

"We work together for eight hours every day and if any one of us is sorely tempted to smoke the others rally round to give encouragement. The continual atmosphere of support and encouragement from your workmates helps a lot. All our other workmates are watching our progress very closely so not one of us dares give in to smoking now!"

QUITTERS' STORIES

Mrs. M. A., mother and housewife . . .

"My 17-year-old daughter was smoking. She promised to stop if I did too. At the same time my 11-year-old son kept coming home from school telling me what he had been taught at school about the dangers of smoking. 'Mummy, I don't want you to die. Please don't smoke those nasty cigarettes...' I stopped for my son's sake and my daughter stopped with me.

"Funny how you'll do things for your kids' sake rather than for your own."

TOBACCO TRIVIA

Here is a selection of 'Tobacco Trivia' questions to test your knowledge, and hopefully, to keep you in a light-hearted mood, whilst you while away your smoke-free hours!

QUESTIONS:

1. What percentage of smokers are hooked before the age of 18 yrs?
a. 5%   b. 20%
c. 35%   d. 75% +

2. Who described smoking as . . . "A custom loathsome to the eye, harmful to the brain, dangerous to the lungs."?

3. How many women smokers manage to give up their cigarettes in pregnancy?
a. 14%   b. 35%   c. 60%

4. What is the major cause of chronic lung disease?

5. How many shots of nicotine per day will the unborn baby receive, if its mother smokes 20 cigarettes a day?

6. How many known or suspected cancer-causing agents are there in cigarette smoke?

7. How many shots of nicotine will that baby have received by the time it is actually born into the world?

8. Is it the nicotine or tar in cigarette smoke that causes cancer?

9. In the U.K. in 1920, men were smoking on average 6 cigarettes per day. How many were they smoking by the late 1980's?

10. How quickly after inhaling tobacco smoke does nicotine reach the brain?
1. Never   2. 7 seconds
3. 7 minutes   4. 15 minutes

ANSWERS:

1. 75% + . 2. King James I. 3. 14% 4. Cigarette smoking. 5. 200 per day. 6. At least 50. 7. 56,000 shots. 8. Tar. 9. 17 cigarettes per day. 10. 7 seconds. Nicotine reaches the brain within 7 seconds of inhaling. That is faster than an intravenous injection of nicotine into the forearm, which would take 14 seconds to reach the brain! A cigarette is a very fast drug delivery system.

Chapter 3

Cash not Ash!

It's not easy to stop smoking and contrary to popular belief the very important health benefits of quitting aren't immediately visible. Quite the opposite, in fact, because the cravings that take over in the first few days can be quite distressing and your new life without cigarettes may make you tense, irritable, depressed and anxious. Your sleep may also be affected.

It's a bleak picture I know, but I'm determined not to pull the wool over your eyes and tempt you into underestimating the task ahead of you. If you can get through the early days, then the health benefits will become apparent and a whole new string of incentives will appear to encourage you to stay a non-smoker.

In the beginning, though, there is one very big and tangible benefit and that is financial. So draw some encouragement from the fact that you are saving money by not smoking and let that steadily growing pile of money strengthen your resolve to continue with the Quit Plan and at the same time take your mind off the distress you might be going through.

Work out how much you are spending on cigarettes each day – and for your own sake do tell the truth. It's remarkable how smokers underestimate the number of cigarettes they smoke when challenged about the scale of their habit.

Once you've calculated how much money you were spending, make a deal with yourself and promise to put the same amount away each day for the foreseeable future.

Now take a clear glass jar and stick a label on it, writing on that label these three words – CASH NOT ASH.

Put the jar in a prominent position – somewhere where you will see it every day. At the end of each day, put the money you would have spent on cigarettes into the jar. Not only is it encouraging to see the cash mounting up, but also you see an immediate and tangible benefit from stopping smoking. Enjoy planning what to do with the money you have saved and treat yourself to a reward for coping with the discomfort of withdrawal. I'll leave it entirely up to you to decide what to buy . . . just as long as it's not cigarettes!

Some former smokers put the money they save into a bank account and eventually spend it on a major treat like a holiday – imagine being able to book a holiday that you otherwise would never have had but for stopping smoking.

If you are working and paying tax on your income, here is an interesting exercise relating to your money and your cigarettes.

You buy your cigarettes with 'take home money'. The money you spend on cigarettes is what you have left in your wages after income tax has been deducted from your gross income. I have worked out the example in brackets as if you smoked 20 cigarettes a day at a cost of £2.25. You should complete the following for the actual number of cigarettes you smoke and the real cost to you:

Cost to You

(A) Each **day** I spend the
following amount on
cigarettes: . . . (£2.25)

(B) Each **week** I spend the
following amount on
cigarettes: . . . (£15.75)

(C) This is money on which
I have had to pay Income
Tax. I pay Income Tax at the
rate of: . . . (25%)

(D) Therefore, before the
deduction of Income Tax, this
sum of money was worth:
[Amount = (B) x 100/75]   . . . (£21.00)

(E) Hence when I stop smoking
I will be increasing my gross
weekly income by: . . . (£21.00)

(F) So by giving up cigarettes I
will be giving myself a wage
increase each **month** of: . . . (£84.00)

(G) This amounts to an annual
     wage increase of: . . . (£1,008.00)

You will therefore be giving yourself an instant wage increase, without having to work extra hours and without having to crawl to the boss with cap in hand. All you have to do is to stop smoking.

Now I want you to do another calculation. I would like you to work out how much money you will spend on cigarettes between now and the day you retire. Fill in your own details in the empty column. As before, I have given you an example in brackets based on a 35-year-old man smoking 20 cigarettes a day:

                                        Cost to You

(1) Age now: . . . (35 yrs)

(2) Retirement age: . . . (65 yrs)

(3) No. of years to retirement: . . . (30 yrs)

(4) Amount spent on cigs/week: . . . (£15.75)
     [See amount (B) above]

(5) Amount spent on cigs/year: . . . (£819.00)
     [52 x amount (4) above]

(6) Amount that will be spent on
     cigs. up to retirement: . . . (£24,570.00)
     [(3) multiplied by (5)]

Remember this calculation is based on cigarettes at today's prices. As they will not stay at today's prices for the next 30 years, the final amount will be a much larger sum of money.

So don't forget:

CASH NOT ASH

On stopping smoking the wealth benefits come first but the health benefits are following close behind.

QUITTERS' STORIES

Mrs. E.B., cleaner ...

"When I stopped smoking previously I never noticed any financial benefit, because the money dwindled away on other unimportant items.

"I used the 'CASH NOT ASH' idea and with the money saved I bought some new furniture – which was badly needed, I can tell you! No one is allowed to smoke anywhere near the new settee or armchairs. I don't want my furniture stinking of smoke or riddled with cigarette burns, no thank you!"

Mrs. T.L., executive ...

"It annoyed me to think that I was spending money and watching it go up in smoke. A great deal of money had literally been burnt at my fingertips.

"I stopped smoking, followed the 'CASH NOT ASH' principle and opened a new savings account for my new source of funds. I told my husband that I had called this new account my 'Nicholas O'Tine' account (Nic. O'Tine ... nicotine – get it?).

"Nicholas O'Tine has a sizeable account to his name now."

Mr. H.O., motorway maintenance ...

"As my wife and I were heavy smokers, we decided to make full use of any savings that ensued from stopping smoking. The money that we were saving each month after stopping smoking equalled the monthly payments on a new car that we had always fancied having.

"We had never had a brand new car before, so we were very excited at our new purchase.

"We dare not go back to smoking now as we couldn't afford to keep up the payments!"

Mrs. J.Mc., teacher ...

"I hadn't been on holiday abroad for years. I needed a holiday badly. So I stopped smoking and put the money into my 'CASH NOT ASH' jar. It was going to take me nearly 12 months to save up all of the money needed for this holiday. That was a good target to aim for. Whenever I felt like having a cigarette I looked at how much I had saved, and thought of my approaching holiday.

"I never smoked, I saved a lot of money and I had a great holiday. It gave me a great sense of achievement and I felt great walking past the duty free shop. I even refused to bring back some duty free cigarettes for my friends."

Section B

Stopping Smoking

Chapter 4

Shift all Cigarettes

Between settling on your Quit Day and actually stopping smoking, there is no need to change your habits. Continue to smoke your usual brand of cigarettes and in the same numbers as before. Cutting down or switching to a milder brand during this period is irrelevant.

Your preparation for a life without smokes should begin on the evening before your Quit Day. Smoke normally until just before bedtime – but from then on it's vital that you remove all remaining cigarettes from the house. Give them away, break them into pieces and throw them in the rubbish bin: I don't mind how you do it just so long as you remove temptation from your path. It can break your heart, I know, to get rid of such beautiful cigarettes but beware of any temptation to hang on to the odd packet for a rainy day. If you do hold on to some cigarettes, then I'm afraid you're not sufficiently motivated to give up smoking and your attitude to quitting is too faint-hearted to have any real chance of success.

Assuming that you are still on course for Quit Day and have gathered up all those remaining cigarettes I'm perfectly happy for you to remove one for a last smoke before putting the rest in the bin. Smoke it and enjoy every puff then go to bed with the memory lingering in your mind, sure in the knowledge that if you can match up to the challenge of the weeks ahead you will emerge as a non-smoker and everything will have seemed well worthwhile.

Get up bright and early on Quit Day – put a spring in your step and enjoy yourself. You're no longer a smoker so you have no need for cigarettes. This means no need for cigarettes in your pockets, your car, your desk or your locker: believe me you'll be glad now that you went to all that trouble to get rid of your remaining cigarettes last night. It's helpful also to remove any of the smoking paraphernalia from around the house. Hide away ashtrays and cigarette lighters so they're not within sight every time temptation comes along. Some quitters have even been known to give away their expensive lighters to friends as an indication of their determination to stop smoking. They argue that the humiliation of having to ask for the lighter back helps strengthen their resolve to kick the habit.

Don't try to put unfair pressure on anyone in your house who is continuing to smoke but ask them politely if they would mind not smoking in your immediate vicinity, perhaps smoking in only one particular room. Encourage them to clean used ashtrays and clear away their cigarette ends. Be careful not to make it seem as though you are trying to impose your new regime on them and I think that generally other smokers will turn out to be supportive of you in your efforts.

Try to give your car a thorough clean a few days before you stop smoking. While doing this, make sure the ashtrays are emptied and search the inside of the car – it's surprising the sort of corners in which that odd cigarette might be hiding. Have a good session with the air freshener and banish those stale smoky smells for good. You'll feel as though you're going to work in a new car on Quit Day morning.

Some smokers say they feel more confident and less anxious if they know they have the odd packet of cigarettes hidden away in a cupboard or drawer. They convince themselves that they don't want to smoke them, arguing that they are there merely to provide psychological support. With no cigarettes around they believe they will panic. On the contrary, I must point out that the quitter who hangs on to the odd packet is playing a very dangerous game ... exposing himself or herself to grave temptations. Imagine an overweight person going on a diet with the fridge stocked up with a mouthwatering selection of fresh cream cakes!

When you stop smoking you know that you will have cravings for cigarettes. These cravings for a smoke can be very troublesome at times and, if you know where some cigarettes are kept, then those cravings will overcome your willpower and you will most likely have a smoke – and most probably you will do that in secret so that no-one knows you have succumbed.

Most smokers, who have tried to give up smoking and failed, admit to going back to smoking under one of the following three circumstances:

(a) As a result of unexpected stress.

(b) After an enjoyable meal.

(c) In association with alcohol.

Previously you always enjoyed cigarettes in the above situations. Your brain was conditioned into expecting a smoke every single time these situations arose. Once you have given up cigarettes your brain will, as a pure reflex, expect you to have a cigarette whenever you find yourself in similar circumstances. If you cannot have a smoke, you will feel a craving that will gnaw at you so badly that you may go looking for a cigarette. If you know where there are some cigarettes then you will be sorely tempted indeed to smoke at least one. That one could be the one that sends you back into smoking.

You may be able to anticipate the food and alcohol situations and, therefore, prepare yourself to cope with them, but you will never be able to anticipate unexpected stress. Stress makes you smoke because in cigarette smoke there is a drug which relaxes you. Very few smokers can cope with stress without lighting a cigarette. Very few ex- smokers could cope with stress without lighting up a cigarette if one was close to hand.

In this book I shall show you how to cope with stress without cigarettes; and, believe me, you will be able to do so. Millions of non-smokers cope with stress without cigarettes and so will you.

So despite any reservations about keeping some cigarettes "in case of an emergency", you *MUST* remove all cigarettes, lighters and ashtrays from your life. This should be done on the night before your Quit Day. After your first couple of weeks without cigarettes you should be able to cope with lighters, ashtrays and cigarettes around you. During that first fortnight you are very vulnerable, so you have to try and help yourself by keeping temptation away.

So many smokers have tried to give up cigarettes and failed just because they did not follow the advice – "shift all cigs"!

GET RID OF ALL CIGARETTES

Now that you have read this chapter, I advise you to ask the smoking members of your family, or your friends at work who smoke, to read it also, so that they will have some understanding of why you'd rather not have cigarettes, ashtrays and lighters around you.

QUITTERS' STORIES

Mrs. K.D., civil servant . . .

"I tried to shift all the cigarettes on the night before Quit Day, but I couldn't be bothered going out to the car to remove the few left in the glove compartment. There they stayed and I completely forgot about them until one day on the way to work I was involved in a minor road accident. The passenger door was badly dented and the other driver admitted liability. I was so badly shaken and upset by the accident that I reached into the glove compartment and had half smoked the cigarette before I realised what I had done. The other driver had lit the cigarette for me to steady my nerves. I could have kicked him! I could have kicked myself too for not getting rid of those few cigarettes, as advised."

Mr. G.J., commercial traveller . . .

"I didn't want to get rid of all my cigarettes, because I normally panic when I know that I haven't got any cigarettes left anywhere. I felt that I would be far more comfortable and confident knowing that I had one or two cigarettes left. In fact, I devised a plan of my own.

I felt very confident that I was going to stop smoking – so confident that I reckoned there was no way that cigarettes were going to get the better of me ever again. I drive a lot each day, so I stuck an unsmoked cigarette onto the inside of my windscreen with sticky tape. As I drove along I talked to that cigarette, saying ... 'OK, we'll see who's going to win this battle. I'm stronger than you, you weed! There's no way that I'm giving in to you.'

"That cigarette stayed there for 3 weeks, and then I had an upsetting argument with one of my customers. I was raging with temper as I drove off and was glad to see that cigarette waiting there on the inside of the windscreen. Before finishing the cigarette I realised my folly ... I wasn't even enjoying smoking it!

"However, despite telling myself that it wasn't enjoyable, I went and bought a packet of cigarettes the following day. I recommenced smoking but happily I later stopped and have not smoked since ... That was 2 years ago. When I stopped then, I certainly did not have any cigarettes on me or in the car at any time."

Chapter 5

Just for Today

We've now reached a crucial stage in the 'Nicotine Phaseout Programme' and this is a good time to take stock. There are three key stages in the overall process of stopping smoking:

★ Preparing to stop

★ Stopping

★ Staying stopped

So far we've worked our way through the first part of the process and we're now into the second part of the programme − getting down to the business of quitting. First of all check your progress to date:

★ Have you named your Quit Day?

★ Have you persuaded someone to quit with you?

★ On the eve of your Quit Day are you prepared to get rid of all your cigarettes?

★ Have you set up your CASH NOT ASH jar?

★ Have you read Chapters 7 to 9 on the various 'NICOTINE PHASEOUT THERAPIES' − and have you obtained the treatment pack of your choice from your local pharmacist? Remember that if you are to use the Nicabate patch or the Nicorette patch you will be starting this on the **MORNING** of your Quit Day. If you are using the Nicotinell patch, you will be putting it on as you go to bed on the **EVE** of your Quit Day.

So far you've shown a great deal of determination, so let's get down to the real business. It's time to draw back the curtains on 'Day One' of your life without the weed, so welcome to your Quit Day.

QUIT DAY   The day you stop smoking forever! Does that fill you with fear or excitement? I should imagine that you must feel rather anxious at the thought of never having a cigarette again. Most smokers when they give up their cigarettes tend to think rather pessimistically about their future.

The idea of never being able to have another cigarette again for the rest of your life is a very depressing thought indeed. The thought of no cigarettes whilst on holiday, or no cigarettes at Christmas, or at this party or that social occasion can make you feel quite depressed. Remember that your cigarette habit has become deeply ingrained into your daily routines. You have always had a smoke with tea or coffee; or after a meal with a drink. You've always bought duty free cigarettes when travelling abroad on holiday and cigarettes have always helped you to cope with new social situations, as well as stressful situations.

Now that you have stopped, how on earth are you going to cope without cigarettes in all these situations throughout the rest of your life?

HERE'S HOW TO MAKE QUITTING AS EASY AS POSSIBLE

Follow my tips when you wake up on the morning of your Quit Day:

★ Do **NOT** think that you have now stopped smoking forever.

★ Do **NOT** tell yourself that you will never ever smoke again.

★ Do **NOT** feel depressed about not having cigarettes at parties, Christmas etc.

★ Do **NOT** tell yourself that you will never be able to enjoy the taste of a cigarette ever again.

Instead of such negative thoughts about no cigarettes forever, you must adopt an attitude of mind that will help you get through each day as easily as possible. You must train your mind into thinking this way:

> "I haven't given up smoking forever.
> All I'm going to do is − I will not have a cigarette **TODAY!**"

> "All that I have to do is get through **THIS DAY** alone without a smoke!"

IN OTHER WORDS DO NOT THINK ANY FURTHER AHEAD THAN TODAY

The task you have to cope with is, not living the rest of your life without cigarettes, but getting through this single first day without a smoke. If you cannot get through one day without smoking − especially your Quit Day − how on earth are you going to cope without cigarettes for the rest of your life?

Surely you can try and get through this single first day without resorting to cigarettes? If it means going to bed tonight at 8.00pm, to get the day out of the way − do it! When you wake up tomorrow morning, you can then proudly say to yourself. . . "I did it! I've gone one full day without a cigarette."

If you can go one day without smoking, you can certainly go one more day. After all, stopping smoking never killed anybody. Whereas continuing to smoke kills thousands upon thousands of people. When, not if, you get through that first day without having a cigarette, you must record your progress on the 'Smoker's Quit Chart', which you will find at the back of this book. A cigarette-free day is recorded by putting a tick on the relevant successful day. Any day after your Quit Day which is not cigarette-free is recorded with a cross. You are now charting your progress, so be honest with yourself and if you have a day where you have sneaked a smoke, then face up to it and put that cross on the chart.

SETTING A QUIT DAY

Don't become despondent if some days are not as successful as others, for, later in the Quit Plan, full guidance and help will be given to you on how to cope with these little slip-ups that do occur during the process of quitting.

As you go through each day trying to manage without cigarettes you will feel the urge to smoke come and go. As each day passes by, you get further and further away from the smoking habit; and as your smoking days become more and more distant so the cravings and thoughts of smoking become less and less troublesome.

Taking **ONE DAY AT A TIME** makes sense, and most successful ex-smokers have adopted this very philosophy of giving up smoking one day at a time. Remember, as I said to you before:

"I haven't given up forever, I just won't have one *today*!"

All I'm asking you to do is —
Get through ONE DAY without a cigarette.

Just convince yourself —
"Just for Today — I won't have a smoke!"

QUITTERS' STORIES

Mr. F.D., sewing machine mechanic...

"If I can't stop smoking for one day only, how on earth can I expect to stay off cigarettes forever? I therefore stop every day for only one day at a time, and it's now 10 months since my last cigarette!"

Mr. G.T., male nurse...

"In the past I've tried to go for one hour without a smoke. Then I tried to go for two hours without a smoke. The problem with that type of approach was that you were waiting for the appointed time to come round just so that you could have your cigarette. You were becoming obsessed with the wait for the next cigarette.

"Getting through one day at a time is far easier to cope with. It's a challenge I can cope with ... not having a cigarette just for today, because maybe tomorrow ... well who knows?"

Mrs.D.B., shop owner...

"I'd hate to think that I could never have a cigarette again. Thinking of not having one just for today is easy. I can cope with dreading just one day at a time."

Miss S.W., receptionist...

"I used to be an alcoholic and I succeeded in giving up the drink by coping with just one day at a time. Then it was 'Just for today, I won't have a drink', now it's 'Just for today, I won't have a smoke.'"

TOBACCO TRIVIA

Here is a selection of 'Tobacco Trivia' questions to test your knowledge, and hopefully, to keep you in a light-hearted mood, whilst you while away your smoke-free hours!

QUESTIONS:

1. Carbon monoxide, a colourless, odourless and poisonous gas, is present at what concentration in cigarette smoke (parts per million)?

a. 10 ppm   b. 50 ppm
c. 150 ppm   d. Over 1000 ppm

2. 75% of smoking children have at least one parent who smokes. True or false?

3. What weight would an ex-smoker have to put on to face the same danger to his life by smoking?

4. When was tobacco discovered on the American Continent?

5. What percentage of the adult population smoke?

a. 12%   b. 55%   c. 30%

6. How does smoking make you look older?

7. By how many minutes does each cigarette shorten the smoker's life?

8. How many people die each year from smoking?

9. If both parents smoke, what is the equivalent number of cigarettes a child or baby in the house would be subjected to – in one year?

a. 0 – 30   b. 40 – 60
c. 70 – 90   d. More than 100

10. Who wrote... "I kissed my first women and smoked my first cigarette on the same day. I have never had time for tobacco since..."?

ANSWERS:

1. 150 ppm. This is the average concentration of carbon monoxide in each mouthful of cigarette smoke that is inhaled. The average smoker will take 10 inhalations of this gas per cigarette. The smoke drifting up into the air from the end of the cigarette, has carbon monoxide at a concentration in excess of 1000 ppm. 2. True 3. 5 stone! 4. About 1495. 5. 30%. Which is nearly one third of the population – 31% of men & 29% of women smoke. 6. By causing premature wrinkling of the skin. 7. 5 minutes. 8. 110,000. That is about 300 people a day, which is equivalent to a fully laden Jumbo jet crashing every other day of the week, and all passengers on board being killed. 9. 70 – 90. If both parents smoke, the levels of nicotine in the baby's body are equivalent to that baby smoking 80 cigarettes per year – that is about one and a half cigarettes per week! 10. Toscanini.

Chapter 6

Nicotine – Nice or Nasty?

Smokers smoke for the effects of nicotine but die from the effects of the other constituents of tobacco, such as tar and carbon monoxide. There are a number of ways in which a fix of nicotine can be taken into the body, the most popular of which is by smoking a cigarette.

GLOBALLY OVER ONE BILLION SMOKERS CONSUME MORE THAN FIVE TRILLION CIGARETTES EACH YEAR.

The smoke from cigarettes is acidic and, when inhaled into the lungs, nicotine is absorbed straight into the bloodstream. Nearly every cigarette smoker inhales because this is the only way to get that rapid fix of nicotine straight into the bloodstream.

Pipe and cigar smokers don't need to inhale to get their fix of nicotine. Unlike that from cigarettes, the smoke from pipes and cigars is alkaline, and this enables nicotine from pipe and cigar smoke to be taken straight into the bloodstream from the lining of the mouth. Lifelong cigar and pipe smokers do not inhale, so they are less likely to suffer from the diseases of the lungs that afflict cigarette smokers, such as emphysema (where the lungs thin like an old sponge) and lung cancer. Heart disease, strokes and circulatory problems are also less common in these types of smokers.

Because of this, most insurance companies treat pipe and cigar smokers as 'non-smokers'. I think this is extremely generous of them, given that pipe and cigar smokers are still prone to cancer of the lip, tongue, mouth and throat.

Now I can imagine that you may be thinking that all you need to do is to change from smoking cigarettes to cigars or a pipe, since that seems a safer option. Unfortunately, this is not the case. Once you have been a cigarette smoker for some time, you will automatically inhale deeply to get your fix of nicotine. If you then change over to smoking cigars or a pipe, you will continue to inhale the smoke – indeed this type of smoke is stronger than the smoke from a cigarette. Many people who try to give up cigarettes only to fail have a tendency to kid themselves that they will only smoke the odd cigar, often after meals and with a comforting drink. This odd cigar becomes five or more a day, so that they are soon in an even more dangerous position than they were when they were smoking cigarettes.

Insurance companies are also very generous in offering discounts on life insurance policies to non-smokers and to ex-smokers. Non-smokers are offered a discount of as much as a third off their premiums – and smokers who stop smoking and stay stopped for 12 months are offered this very attractive discount. So if this book works for you and you stop smoking for 12 months, you should contact your insurance company to negotiate a handsome reduction in your premium.

In fact this discount to the non-smoker is not what it seems. In reality it amounts to a 50 per cent loading on the premium a smoker has to pay for the same cover as a non-smoker. This simple example will demonstrate the point:

> Imagine a smoker applies for life insurance and his annual premium comes to a total of £150. I, as a non-smoker, apply for exactly the same insurance cover, and given that we are similar in age and weight and are both reasonably healthy, I will receive the non-smoking discount of a third. My premium is thereby reduced by £50, so I will only pay £100. You can see how the smoker is in fact paying 50 per cent more for the same life insurance cover.

There is good reason for this: smoking is dangerous to health and smokers are known to be at a higher risk of dying prematurely because of their habit. How many smokers realise the following rather frightening statistic:

40 per cent of smokers DO NOT live to collect their pension.
They die before retirement.

Your response might be, "Well, what about non-smokers? How many of them die before retirement?" The answer is 15 per cent. Smoking really does cause premature death and the insurance companies really do know their business – and they are not in the business of throwing money away.

OTHER
SOURCES
OF NICOTINE

Snuff. This is powdered tobacco, which is often available in different flavours such as menthol and mentholyptus. There is even a 'medicated snuff', which gives the misleading impression that it might be healthy to take it. Snuff is taken as a fine powder, a pinch between finger and thumb being sniffed up into each nostril. The fine tobacco powder then delivers its fix of nicotine through the lining of the nose into the bloodstream. It's rather interesting that other drugs which affect the mind are also snorted, such as cocaine and glue.

Stoppers. These are small tablets sold as 'tobacco substitute lozenges', which can be bought over the counter in chemists' shops. They are said to contain 'purified tobacco – free from harmful resins and tars'! I'm not too sure what that means, but if there is tobacco in the lozenge, then it will contain nicotine, which will be released into the bloodstream as it dissolves against the inside of the mouth. The lozenge should not be chewed, sucked or swallowed.

Skoal Bandits. These are small pouches which contain shredded tobacco. They actually look like miniature tea bags, and are intended to be placed in the mouth and rested between the cheek and the gum. As the 'tobacco tea bag' becomes saturated with saliva, the tobacco 'juice' is released into the mouth, and so nicotine is absorbed through the lining of the mouth into the bloodstream. This method of nicotine delivery is rather similar to that of the nicotine chewing gum, Nicorette, which releases its nicotine upon being chewed. However, nicotine gum is safe in that it contains only pure nicotine at low doses and does not cause cancer, because there is no tobacco in it. 'Skoal Bandits', on the other hand, contain tobacco which not only releases nicotine into the mouth but also substances known to cause cancer. As cigarettes can cause lung cancer, so this oral tobacco can cause cancer of the mouth, and, in America, there have been cases of mouth cancer occurring even in young people who have used this type of tobacco product.

Resolution. This is sold in chemists' shops as an anti-smoking lozenge. Its active ingredients are purified nicotine, Vitamin A, Vitamin C and Vitamin E. The lozenges are sucked in place of cigarettes and, in a similar way to Nicorette and Stoppers, are said to release nicotine into the bloodstream through the lining of the mouth. As there is no tobacco in this product, there is no danger of oral cancer developing as a result of using it.

Chewing tobacco. The use of chewing tobacco is quite rare in this country today. But for those who use it, the risks of developing mouth cancer are very real indeed. The 'Skoal Bandits' mentioned above are really just a more socially acceptable way of using oral tobacco as a means of getting nicotine into the body, as well as all the cancer causing substances.

IS THERE A PERFECT CIGARETTE?

As smokers smoke for nicotine, but unfortunately die from the effects of inhaled tar, carbon monoxide and many of the other chemicals in tobacco smoke, it might seem a pity that you can't get a 'nicotine only' cigarette.

A few years ago an American company, called *Advanced Tobacco Products,* produced a smokeless cigarette called 'Favor'. This looked exactly like a cigarette but was in fact a plastic tube containing a sponge-like foam impregnated with nicotine. The 'cigarette' was not lit and so did not produce any smoke. All you had to do was to inhale upon the 'cigarette' and you received a dose of nicotine which you breathed down into your lungs, where it was then absorbed into the bloodstream and carried to the brain. Once the brain received its 'fix' of nicotine the craving for a smoke was satisfied.

In other words it was not unlike having a real cigarette, in that nicotine got to the brain within seven seconds of inhaling; and once there, the nicotine had the same effect as nicotine from tobacco smoke – but without the dangers associated with tobacco smoke. So this was a safer way of getting your nicotine, while still having the ritual hand to mouth activity associated with the use of real cigarettes.

This would seem a relatively safe way of obtaining nicotine and indeed smokers who tried it found that it was quite an acceptable substitute for a real cigarette. However, the product is no longer available and there are several rumours about its withdrawal from the market. Some people believe that the US Government withdrew it because it was seen as a real threat to cigarettes which are a major source of revenue; moreover, as it did not contain any tobacco, they could not slap tobacco tax upon it.

It is also rumoured that a drug company has actually bought the product and is perfecting it as an ethical medical treatment, to be available on prescription. This would give us a rather novel means of delivering nicotine into the body for smokers who want to give up smoking – we shall see in time.

Other methods of delivering nicotine into the body are currently being researched. Within a couple of years a nicotine nasal spray will become available as a stop-smoking treatment – quite an improvement on the old fashioned snuff! You just 'snort' your nicotine instead of lighting up. A nicotine inhaler is also being evaluated along lines similar to the inhalers used by asthmatics. The nicotine will be delivered as a fine mist from a small aerosol, as the patient inhales from the spray. This will closely mimic the delivery of nicotine from a cigarette and its effect will be felt just as rapidly – without any dangerous tobacco smoke.

How very resourceful man has been with regard to delivering this drug into the body. We have cigarettes, cigars, pipes, chewing tobacco, snuff, 'tobacco tea bags', tobacco lozenges, nicotine chewing gum and nicotine skin patches – which will be discussed later. What next?

Nicotine suppositories? You may well laugh, but we do know that nicotine is well absorbed across the lining of the anus and rectum into the bloodstream. Doesn't that make you wonder just how on earth someone discovered that? The mind boggles!

In high doses nicotine can be dangerous, causing nausea, vomiting and muscular paralysis. Obviously, these dangerous levels are never achieved during normal smoking, but do you remember the feelings of nausea you experienced when you first started smoking? At that time you weren't accustomed to the drug and even small doses adversely affected you, yet you persevered to overcome those side-effects. Why? Because your friends smoked and it was the 'in thing' to do. If you didn't smoke you weren't part of the crowd or one of the gang. If you did smoke you were 'grown up' and mature.

THE ADDICTION TRAP

So you made yourself smoke despite the unpleasant effects, and then you developed a 'taste' or a desire for the cigarette. When you hadn't had one for some time you noticed a craving developing. This, you now realised, was especially noticeable first thing in the morning, because you had been without a cigarette for eight hours and your blood nicotine levels were very low.

In fact, research has now shown that once an adolescent has smoked 4 cigarettes he or she is usually addicted for life — and this is what I mean by the addiction trap. Could anything more clearly demonstrate the power of the drug, when only 4 cigarettes trap you into a lifelong addiction!

Nicotine has two pleasant effects upon the body. First of all, in small doses, it acts as a stimulant — giving you a lift when you are feeling down or bored. Secondly, in larger doses, it does just the opposite — it calms you down and relaxes you. Very few drugs are capable of having two such different and opposing effects upon the body. Not only does nicotine have these nice effects on how your body feels, it also acts very quickly upon your brain. Within 7 seconds of inhaling the cigarette smoke, nicotine is already entering the brain cells — this is faster than actually injecting nicotine directly into your bloodstream, because an injection of nicotine into a vein takes 14 seconds to reach the brain.

This is because the lungs have an incredible ability to absorb it from inhaled smoke and the transit time from the lungs to the brain is very short.

IS SMOKING A REAL DRUG ADDICTION?

The World Health Organisation's definition of addiction is as follows:

> "The compulsion to take a drug, on a continuous basis, in order to experience its effects, or to avoid the discomfort of its absence."

Amongst the 4,000 chemicals identified in tobacco smoke, we know that nicotine is the drug the smoker is seeking. A smoker takes about 10 puffs per cigarette, so the average smoker of 20 cigarettes a day is taking into his or her body 200 puffs of nicotine-laden smoke every day. On stopping smoking smokers feel tense, aggressive, depressed; they may suffer from insomnia, loss of concentration, cravings for cigarettes, and, in many, weight gain becomes a problem. If you are still in any doubt whether smoking fits the WHO definition of an addictive drug, read on:

> "The compulsion to take a drug (nicotine), on a continuous basis (200 fixes per day), in order to experience its effects (relaxant and stimulant), or to avoid the discomfort of its absence (tension, aggression, depression, insomnia, loss of concentration, cravings, weight gain)."

Still not convinced?

Take a look at the Italian experience.

THE ITALIAN EXPERIENCE – '92

In November 1992 there was a strike of 14,000 employees of the Italian state tobacco monopoly. This caused such a great cigarette shortage that within three weeks, respectable citizens were competing with small boys for cigarette butts thrown onto the pavement. People even snatched cigarettes dangling from people's mouths, and one unfortunate individual was arrested in Florence when he rushed up to a smoker and held a knife to his throat, demanding a cigarette. When most tobacconists closed down, women resorted to smoking cigars and pipes.

THE ITALIAN EXPERIENCE '92

Apparently, huge traffic jams formed as thousands of desperate smokers tried to cross the borders into France, Switzerland and Austria to buy cigarettes, some having travelled hundreds of miles to do so.

THE REAL NATURE OF THE PROBLEM

Almost everyone using tobacco could be classed as a nicotine addict. Some smokers are only very slightly addicted while others are more severely addicted. A very small number who only smoke the odd 'social' cigarette are not addicted at all. The slightly addicted are those who are able to give up without any real discomfort, whilst the heavily addicted can't give up their cigarettes despite suffering severe disease caused by their smoking, for example, leg amputation due to gangrene.

Indeed, the addiction to nicotine is so deep-rooted and the erosion of a smoker's willpower is so overwhelming that he or she is unable to give up tobacco permanently, even after life-threatening and serious conditions caused by their smoking. For example, 50 per cent of smokers who manage to give up their cigarettes after surviving a major heart attack return to smoking within just 6 months. A similar relapse rate applies to smokers who develop cancer of the larynx or voice box.

Imagine having your voice box removed because you have developed cancer as a direct result of cigarette smoking. You are unable to speak and you have to learn to form words by 'belching up' air from your stomach. Can you believe that even after that horrific experience, 50 per cent of those patients are back smoking again within 6 months of surgery!

Cigarettes are the most popular source of nicotine, and there are 14 million adult cigarette smokers in Great Britain today. Other sources of nicotine are snuff and chewing tobacco, neither of which are currently very popular in this country. About one in three men and women smoke and, tragically, young girls are taking up the habit even more avidly than young boys.

Such has been the increase in smoking amongst women, which started after World War II, that smoking-related diseases are now taking their toll –

AND LUNG CANCER IS NOW OVERTAKING BREAST CANCER AS THE MAIN CAUSE OF CANCER DEATHS IN WOMEN.

Although the total number of adult smokers is slowly decreasing, the total number of cigarettes being sold is not decreasing: this can only mean that individual smokers are smoking more cigarettes. Doctors, who were once heavily addicted, have been successful in quitting smoking and today no more than 10 per cent of the medical profession smoke. And why? Because we see in our everyday work every horrific consequence of cigarette smoking.

Not only does smoking kill prematurely, but those who are lucky enough to avoid an unexpected early death often have their quality of life severely affected by diseases such as chronic bronchitis and emphysema. Such patients may develop severe shortness of breath whilst just washing or shaving in the mornings. They need oxygen in their home and can be so severely afflicted that they are unable to walk outside their front doors. They become prisoners within their own homes, spending most of their time just fighting to get the next breath.

WHY DOES NICOTINE CAUSE ADDICTION?

Nicotine is a psychoactive drug – in other words it works primarily on the chemistry of the brain. Watch a smoker under stress and notice how he or she deeply inhales a large volume of smoke right down into the lungs, holding it there for a few seconds and then exhaling, before rapidly repeating the same ritual. This large volume of smoke delivers a **large** shot of nicotine, which quickly **relaxes** the smoker.

Isn't it interesting how the smoker is totally unaware that he or she is adjusting the dose of nicotine he or she needs at that precise moment?

A bored smoker, with nothing else to do, will take small puffs on his cigarette, to self administer **small** doses of nicotine for its **stimulating** effects. So in the course of smoking, not only is nicotine reaching the brain in 7 seconds, but it is also having different and totally opposite effects, depending upon the dose the smoker requires at that precise moment in time.

Nicotine slows down the activity of the stomach – so that a cigarette after a meal is a very enjoyable experience, because the smoker feels replete and satisfied. There is also a suppression of your appetite with nicotine, so when you stop smoking your appetite improves. Nicotine stimulates the activity of the bowel so a smoker often moves his or her bowels after the first cigarette of the day. This also explains why smokers often become constipated after stopping smoking.

Nicotine improves concentration and short-term memory. This becomes very obvious when a smoker stops smoking – he or she finds it difficult to concentrate on mental tasks. For example when writers and journalists give up smoking they find it extremely difficult to do their job of composing written material, especially when working against a deadline. Nicotine has a slight action in elevating your internal chemistry or metabolism, so it helps you to burn off calories. When you stop smoking, you don't burn off the calories as quickly, so that you may well put on weight. I shall help you avoid that later in this book.

Nicotine and alcohol work together, each enhancing the effects of the other. This is one of the reasons you may enjoy a cigarette with a drink. When you stop smoking, having a drink in the pub or at a party may not seem as enjoyable. Many smokers admit that they started smoking again in circumstances where alcohol was involved. So do be on your guard in social situations, where the alcohol is flowing. We all know how an increasing level of alcohol weakens the ex-smoker's resolve!

So with all these wonderful effects it's not surprising that nicotine causes addiction, especially when cigarettes, cigars and pipe tobacco are legal, relatively cheap and easily obtainable.

ARE THE DANGERS OF SMOKING LESS IF THE SMOKER DOES NOT INHALE OR SMOKES LOW TAR CIGARETTES?

As mentioned previously, virtually every cigarette smoker inhales. The way to deliver nicotine from the cigarette into the brain is to deliver it deep into the lungs, where it is rapidly tranferred to the bloodstream, and carried within seconds to the brain.

Most smokers smoke their cigarettes to achieve their own personal comfort level of nicotine in the blood. Give a smoker a cigarette that is milder than their normal brand and they will smoke that cigarette harder and quicker to get more nicotine out of it – in other words, they are compensating for the weaker 'smoke'. It's as if the smoker has a regulating centre (like a thermostat) in the brain which is set at a certain level, just right for that smoker. So changing to milder brands or even smoking fewer cigarettes each day is not the way to make smoking safer – the only way to make smoking safer is to STOP SMOKING!

WHAT ARE THE POSSIBLE SYMPTOMS OF NICOTINE WITHDRAWAL?

Most smokers experience disturbing, uncomfortable feelings when they have to go for a period of time without their cigarettes –

"I dislike smoking, and I smoke only because not smoking distresses me!"

Bertrand Russell, philosopher.

They commonly suffer from feeling tense, irritable, aggressive, irrational, suffer sleep disturbance, loss of concentration, memory impairment, increased appetite, weight gain, constipation, depression and of course cravings for cigarettes.

Most of these symptoms would not be relieved by giving them cigarettes which contain no nicotine, such as herbal cigarettes, yet instant relief would be afforded by allowing them their normal cigarettes to relieve their nicotine withdrawal symptoms!

Stopping smoking is easy, but staying stopped is difficult because of the very distressing symptoms of nicotine withdrawal, superimposed upon the discomfort of just missing the ritual or habit of lighting up at certain times through the day.

The Department of Health tells us that 70 per cent of adult smokers have tried at least twice to stop and failed. Patients who suffer from smoking-related diseases find it very difficult to stay off their cigarettes, despite grotesque damage to their body.

For example, having had one leg amputated because of gangrene caused by smoking, many smokers continue to smoke, sadly to develop further gangrene in their other leg which has to be amputated. What a bleak introduction to your retirement years – in a wheelchair with both legs amputated above the knees!

Advice from doctors and other such professionals produces low success rates in smoking cessation, mainly because we are not adequately addressing the real nature of the problem – that for very many people the habit of smoking involves a true drug addiction to nicotine.

We surely would not expect a heroin addict to give up his addiction purely upon the advice that he should stop using his drug because it might kill him. It simply wouldn't work. The addiction to nicotine is just as severe, so it is simple common sense that smokers, like all other addicts, need more than just words to enable them to give it up.

WHAT ABOUT HYPNOSIS, ACUPUNCTURE ETC?

Unfortunately hypnosis, acupuncture, behaviour modification, aversion therapy, homeopathy and other similar interventions with smokers have not produced good long-term success rates. At one year follow-up, the best results show success rates of about 15 per cent.

These treatments do not adequately address the problem of addiction to nicotine. When real help, based upon a scientific understanding of nicotine addiction, is given to ease the patient off their addictive drug, then success rates really do improve. New therapies have just become freely available that will help any smoker to stop smoking – and this is the fundamental new message of this book.

Such interventions involve the use of nicotine reduction therapy. With this type of approach the patient tackles the problem in TWO STAGES:

★ 1: Abruptly give up the habit/ritual of smoking, whilst still receiving a small intake of pure nicotine, to avoid nicotine withdrawal symptoms.

★ 2: After 3 months give up the nicotine replacement gradually, using a reducing dose regime.

TOBACCO TRIVIA

Here is a selection of 'Tobacco Trivia' questions to test your knowledge, and hopefully, to keep you in a light-hearted mood, whilst you while away your smoke-free hours!

QUESTIONS:

1. What was the most successful cigarette advertising campaign in history?

2. How many cigarettes does it take to get 94% of teenagers addicted to tobacco for life?

3. Where else is carbon monoxide found besides in cigarette smoke?

4. Red blood cells absorb carbon monoxide 200 times faster than oxygen – true or false?

5. How large an area would the interior surface of the lungs cover?

1. Coffee table   3. Swimming pool
2. Dining table   4. Tennis court

6. How quickly does damage occur after smoking a cigarette?

1. 5 seconds   3. 6 months
2. 1 week   4. 10 years

7. What risk of developing lung cancer and heart disease does the non-smoking spouse of a smoker have?

8. What percentage of smokers would like to give up smoking?

9. What are the odds of a teenager becoming a smoker in a home where no one smokes?

ANSWERS:

1. The Marlboro Country advertisements. 2. Four cigarettes only. 3. In car exhaust fumes. 4. True. 5. Tennis court. This large area of spongey lung tissue exposes the blood vessels to the incoming air and smoke. The lungs then efficiently absorb oxygen from the air and many chemicals from the cigarette smoke. Carbon dioxide passes out of the blood, and is breathed out of the lungs as you exhale. 6. 5 seconds. There are 4,000 chemicals in cigarette smoke, some are very toxic and some are powerful irritants, which soon attack the delicate tissues of your mouth, throat, larynx, and lungs. Many of these chemicals can be carried around the body to affect distant organs such as the kidneys and bladder. 7. Twice the averge risk. 8. 70%. 9. Less than 1 in 20.

Chapter 7

The Nicotine Phaseout Programme – What It's All About

During 15 years in the business of smoking cessation, I have kept an open mind while testing most of the stop-smoking treatments that have been offered to smokers, both here and abroad. Of all the assorted therapies my patients have tried (and there have been many), the use of pure nicotine in small doses, such as in the nicotine chewing gum and the nicotine skin patches, has produced the best long-term results. Success rates are greatly improved when these nicotine preparations are used. No wonder such treatments are becoming more and more popular as smokers try them and find that they really can succeed in quitting!

In the following chapters I shall give you all the help you will need to take maximum advantage of these new and very successful treatments. I shall explain what these new treatments have to offer. Are there any side-effects, for example? I shall deal with this too. But first let us look at how we can spot false claims and promises.

TELLING THE TRUTH – OR WHEN IS A CURE NOT A CURE?

Over the years many types of treatment have attempted to help smokers quit the habit. These have included hypnosis, acupuncture, aversion therapy, behaviour modification, tranquillisers, anti-depressants, psychological procedures, mouth washes, gargles, mouth sprays, records, audio cassettes, video cassettes, scare tactics, public health campaigns, booklets, leaflets and so on.

The effectiveness of any stop-smoking treatment is shown by its cure rate. We define the cure rate as that percentage of smokers who are still not smoking one year after receiving their treatment. Contrary to some rather wild claims, none of the above techniques has produced a proven cure rate greater than 15 per cent after one year of follow-up.

"CUTTING DOWN TO ONE CIGARETTE A DAY IS NOT QUITTING!"

In the scientific assessment of stop-smoking treatments, it's important to verify the truth when smokers say they have stopped smoking. Smoking is a powerful addiction and people who try and fail to give it up are tempted to kid their therapists that they have succeeded. As a result of this, exaggerated claims have been made for less scientifically controlled treatments, alleging they can cure virtually every smoker. One way really to prove that a treatment has been successful is to ask the ex-smoker if he or she will agree to a special test. Measuring the concentration of the carbon monoxide in the ex-smoker's breath is an accurate way of proving whether or not they are still smoking. I am not, of course, suggesting you need to go to these lengths as part of my programme. But some people like to see how quickly they are benefitting from quitting and for this reason they like to have their carbon monoxide levels measured before and after quitting. Simple yet effective machines which measure carbon monoxide levels are now available to doctors. Your GP or practice nurse might even have one of these carbon monoxide monitors, which are known as 'Smokerlysers'.

Now you have a pretty good idea what questions to ask when you see some anti-smoking treatments boasting an exaggerated cure rate of say 90 per cent:

(1) Was that the percentage of smokers who were still off cigarettes one year after receiving treatment or was it just the initially high number who gave up for a very short time? After all, nearly all smokers can give up for very short periods but usually fail in the long term.

(2) Was it proven that they really had given up smoking in the longer term by scientifically verifying this using a test such as the 'Smokerlyser'?

If these questions are not answered at all or if the answer to one or both of these questions is no, then your common sense will tell you where the truth lies.

ATTACKING THE REAL ADDICTION TO TOBACCO

Most treatments are aimed at helping the smoker overcome the **HABIT** of smoking. They do not produce exciting cure rates on their own because they ignore the fact that smoking is not only a habit but it is also an **ADDICTION.** If you don't treat both the habit aspect and the addiction aspect, then you will never achieve good success rates.

Of the thousands of chemicals present in tobacco smoke, nicotine is the only one which is known to be addictive. You smoke to get the drug nicotine into your brain, because it produces some very pleasant effects in the brain cells. As has been mentioned earlier, when taken in small doses, such as little puffs on the cigarette, nicotine acts as a stimulant on the nervous system – in other words it gives you a pleasant sensation of excitement. When taken in larger doses, such as large volumes of smoke inhaled deeply, nicotine acts as a relaxant or tranquilliser.

Remember that example of the smoker under stress – for example the woman waiting for a job interview? See how deeply she inhales the smoke and then holds it in her lungs! High blood levels of nicotine are produced and these bring about the relaxing effect that is so desired when under stress.

No other constituent of cigarette smoke produces these effects upon the smoker. The fundamental importance of nicotine to the smoker is shown by some very interesting research studies.

★ Smokers smoke to achieve a certain level of nicotine in their blood. When the nicotine level falls below a certain level, they feel the desire to smoke.

★ If their cigarettes are treated to remove some of the nicotine, they smoke more cigarettes.

★ If their cigarettes are treated to raise the level of nicotine, they smoke fewer cigarettes.

★ If smokers are given nicotine intravenously or as nicotine gum or nicotine skin patches, and then asked to stop smoking completely, they find that quitting is easier.

The symptoms that trouble smokers on giving up cigarettes are well recognised:

Anxiety	Headache
Irritability	Drowsiness
Difficulty concentrating	Constipation
Restlessness	Craving for tobacco
Depression	Aggression
Weight gain	

Most of these distressing symptoms can be relieved by taking nicotine on its own. Relief of this tobacco withdrawal state is not brought about by any of the other constituents of tobacco smoke, such as tar, carbon monoxide or any of the other 4,000 chemicals present in the smoke. Nor are these symptoms relieved by smoking nicotine-free cigarettes, such as herbal or tobacco-free cigarettes.

WHY USE NICOTINE TO STOP SMOKING?

When you give up cigarettes you suffer from two problems:

(1) You miss the presence of cigarettes in your life. You miss having cigarettes after meals, or with your tea or coffee or with your glass of wine or beer etc. This is the HABIT of smoking that you are missing.

So PROBLEM ONE is withdrawing from the HABIT of smoking.

(2) You miss the drug nicotine that was in your cigarettes. As explained before, nicotine had pleasant effects upon you. You miss those pleasant effects and that's why you're dying for a cigarette. This is the ADDICTION to smoking that you are missing.

So PROBLEM TWO is withdrawing from the ADDICTION of smoking.

TO BECOME A SUCCESSFUL EX-SMOKER YOU MUST TACKLE ONE PROBLEM AT A TIME

Success at giving up smoking is much more likely if you tackle the problem in two stages:

STAGE 1 – You will solve the HABIT problem first. You do this by adhering to all the advice given so far in points 1 to 5 and points 7 and 8 of the 'Smoker's Ten Point Quit Plan'. By doing this you can learn to live without cigarettes in your life.

You should do this whilst still supporting your addiction to nicotine by using either nicotine gum or a nicotine skin patch. Learning to give up just the habit of smoking is bad enough, but trying to give up the habit and at the same time suffering the distress of nicotine withdrawal (with its associated anxiety, irritability etc), can be very unpleasant.

It makes sense to prevent any nicotine withdrawal symptoms by taking nicotine on its own (without dangerous smoke), so that it is easier to learn to live without the cigarettes in your daily routine. At a later stage when you feel that you have completely got rid of the habit of smoking, you can wean yourself off the addictive drug nicotine by gradually reducing your intake of nicotine. You have then got rid of your addiction to smoking.

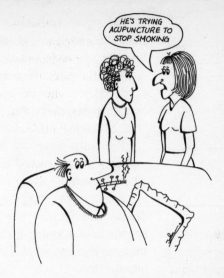

WHAT DO I MEAN BY 'THE NICOTINE PHASEOUT PROGRAMME'?

In my nicotine phaseout programme I pay full attention to both the habit of and the addiction to smoking. I have included many tips that have been gleaned the hard way, from my 15 years of experience in helping many thousands of smokers. In this way, I can honestly promise you the best possible chance of success in your wish to quit smoking – and to stay stopped permanently.

In order to achieve this success, I make full use of the latest scientific advances.

The use of nicotine in preparations such as chewing gum or skin patches to help smokers to stop smoking is usually called 'nicotine replacement therapy'. However, I prefer to call it 'nicotine phaseout therapy', because it neither replaces all the nicotine you were getting from your cigarettes, nor does it aim to replace the nicotine long-term: just over a short period, during which you are weaned off the addiction to nicotine.

This gradually reducing dose of nicotine does have beneficial effects in that it takes the edge off the craving for cigarettes and also helps with many of the other withdrawal symptoms, such as irritability, anxiety, aggression and weight gain. Because you are gradually weaning yourself off nicotine, the addictive drug is slowly 'phased out' of your life – hence this is an important ingredient in the highly successful overall programme – 'THE NICOTINE PHASEOUT PROGRAMME'.

Currently there are two types of nicotine phaseout therapy available – a chewing gum and nicotine patches.

I shall be devoting the next two chapters to a detailed description of how to obtain the maximum benefit from nicotine gum and nicotine patches respectively, so what follows is just a brief introduction.

At present there is only one form of nicotine gum available in the UK. This is called 'Nicorette' and I have had the opportunity to evaluate its effectiveness for 13 years. Nicotine skin patch therapy will be new to many of my readers, though some patches have now been tested on very large numbers of smokers with considerable success and an excellent record of safety. Three brands of nicotine skin patch are now available in the UK, 'Nicabate', 'Nicorette' and 'Nicotinell' patches. A fourth type of skin patch, 'Niconil' is as yet only available in Southern Ireland, though it may be available in the UK soon.

HE ONLY STARTED SMOKING TO BE ONE OF THE CROWD.

Other forms of nicotine delivery systems are also being researched, such as a nicotine nasal spray and a nicotine inhaler.

THE NICOTINE PHASEOUT PROGRAMME – WHY IT IS MY CHOICE OF TREATMENT

Anybody who changes over from cigarettes to nicotine chewing gum or a nicotine skin patch is undergoing a controlled withdrawal which begins with a dramatic fall in his or her daily intake of nicotine. This is then gradually reduced further until, usually over a period of about three months, the smoker has actually 'phased' nicotine out of his or her life – he or she has become a successful long-term non-smoker.

This 'phaseout' of nicotine addiction, coupled with a simultaneous phasing out of the habit aspects of smoking, has proved to be a very useful approach for the many thousands of patients who have attended my Smokers' Clinics.

THE INTRODUCTION OF NICOTINE PHASEOUT THERAPY HAS ACTUALLY DOUBLED THE CHANCES OF SUCCESS FOR MY PATIENTS, AND SO THIS TYPE OF TREATMENT HAS TO BE CONSIDERED SERIOUSLY BY SMOKERS WHO ARE DETERMINED TO GIVE UP SMOKING IN THE LONG TERM.

While phaseout therapy cannot be the perfect solution to nicotine addiction – the perfect solution would be 100 per cent successful – it is by far the most effective solution available today. As no other forms of treatment can produce such high cure rates, the use of nicotine patch therapy must be seriously considered by any smoker wishing to give up cigarettes long-term. This is why I have made this the focus of my nicotine phaseout programme.

TWO FACTS TO REMEMBER

★ Nicotine does not cause cancer. In a healthy individual and at the doses taken in cigarettes, nicotine by itself does not appear to cause any disease other than a powerful addiction; but, when combined with carbon monoxide from tobacco smoke, it is implicated in the production of heart disease, strokes and gangrene.

★ It appears that smokers are smoking for the pleasant effects of the drug nicotine, but dying from the bad effects of tar, carbon monoxide and the other dangerous chemicals in cigarette smoke.

When you replace smoking with the nicotine phaseout treatments described in the following chapters, it will be difficult if not impossible for your body to obtain the same daily intake of nicotine you previously obtained from your cigarettes. So do feel reassured that whatever nicotine replacement therapy you decide to use, you will be getting very low doses of nicotine into the brain, but enough to keep you reasonably 'sane' whilst you learn to live without tobacco in your life. No longer will you be insulting your brain and body with all the noxious chemicals found in tobacco smoke.

The complete process will take about 3 months. Not a long time when you consider that you have probably been smoking for most of your adult life!

You will, then, have kicked the lifelong 'habit' of smoking cigarettes and the lifelong 'addiction' to the drug nicotine. Following this you will feel extremely confident and relieved at accomplishing such a difficult task.

You will be FREE, and if you have also been successful at losing weight with the 'FAT FAREWELL' SLIMMING PLAN, you will be feeling very confident and positive indeed about your own future.

Chapter 8

Nicotine Gum

Nicotine gum was the first of the nicotine replacement therapies. If you would like to know more about it, this chapter may help you. If you would prefer to concentrate on the new skin patch nicotine replacement therapies, please move on directly to the following chapter.

WHAT IS NICOTINE GUM?

Nicotine gum (known in the USA as 'nicotine polacrilex resin') is a chewing gum which contains the drug nicotine. It does not contain any other constituent from tobacco, and therefore, it does NOT cause cancer, as tobacco might, if chewed in the mouth.

The only brand of nicotine chewing gum available is 'Nicorette'. It is available in two strengths, 2mg and 4mg. In the UK, the 2mg gum can be bought over the counter at all pharmacists. The 4mg gum is called 'Nicorette Plus' but at present is only available with a private prescription from your GP.

When used correctly, nicotine gum is extremely useful in controlling the craving for a smoke as well as controlling the other distressing effects felt on stopping smoking, such as anxiety, loss of concentration, irritability, headache and even weight gain.

Some smokers may have already tried nicotine gum without success. When I have questioned people about this, they have often told me that precise instructions on how to use the gum were not given to them. They were not told how many pieces to use per day, nor how often to use the gum. They were not taught the correct chewing technique and so they developed side-effects such as sore throat, indigestion or foul taste in the mouth. All these problems are the result of incorrect use of the nicotine gum.

In my Stop Smoking clinics, patients who have stopped using gum because of problems are encouraged to try it again under more precise guidance, with special emphasis on chewing technique and correct daily dosage. If you have also been disappointed with the gum, I would suggest you try it again following the precise instructions given in this chapter.

HOW TO USE NICOTINE GUM

Nicotine gum is not a wonder cure – but it does make stopping smoking easier. Most doctors will be only too pleased that you are trying to stop smoking and will be happy to give you any assistance you need.

But do remember to have the nicotine gum in your possession before your planned Quit Day. Do not start using it until the morning of your Quit Day. Can you please also note the following, because it is important:

NEVER SMOKE CIGARETTES AND CHEW NICOTINE GUM AT THE SAME TIME.

You should do one or the other. As you are stopping smoking completely from the moment you wake up on your Quit Day, you should use nicotine gum as your only source of nicotine.

HOW THE GUM WORKS

When nicotine gum is chewed, nicotine is released into the mouth where most of it is absorbed through the lining of the mouth into the bloodstream. As chewing continues more and more nicotine is released and the blood levels of nicotine rise. The nicotine travels in the bloodstream around the body and of course reaches the cells of the brain. When the brain receives its nicotine, the need or desire to smoke subsides and the craving goes away.

The gum does not produce levels of nicotine in the blood equivalent to smoking levels. At best the peak level of nicotine produced in the bloodstream by chewing one piece of nicotine gum (2mg strength) is only one third of the level produced by smoking a cigarette.

On stopping smoking and starting nicotine gum, you are already weaning yourself off the drug nicotine – you have started the 'Nicotine Phaseout Programme'. Always remember that in terms of nicotine blood levels:

One piece of nicotine gum = 1/3 of a cigarette.

If you chew twelve pieces of gum each day, you are taking the equivalent in terms of nicotine of only 4 cigarettes. Not only have you drastically reduced your total intake of nicotine but you have also avoided tobacco smoke with its tar, carbon monoxide and 4,000 other dangerous chemicals. Let me stress again that nicotine gum does not cause cancer of the mouth, nor does it cause any serious disease or illness in an otherwise healthy individual.

It never ceases to amaze me how smokers seem to have exaggerated worries about the possible dangers of nicotine gum, which is a very safe product, and yet seem hardly concerned about the dangers they face from having smoked 220,000 cigarettes (20 a day for 30 years).

CAN NICOTINE GUM ITSELF BE ADDICTIVE?

This is a very reasonable question to ask – after all the very reason you have not been able to stop smoking is your addiction to the nicotine present in the cigarette tobacco. If cigarettes were addictive because of their nicotine content, then surely the gum must be just as addictive? Fortunately this is not the case, for some very good reasons:

★ Cigarettes give an immediate effect. Nicotine from cigarette smoke reaches the brain within 7 seconds of inhaling. Nicotine from the gum takes a lot longer to reach the brain, and so the benefit is not felt immediately.

★ The blood levels of nicotine produced by the gum are much lower than those produced by cigarettes. Your total daily dose of nicotine is reduced by using the gum, so you are actually taking less of the addictive drug.

★ On smoking a cigarette you get a surge of nicotine in the bloodstream and it is believed that smokers smoke to get that 'peak' of nicotine in the blood. With nicotine gum there is no surge of nicotine in the blood and the smoker doesn't get a nicotine 'peak'. The gum produces a slow steady rise in blood nicotine levels without any high 'peaks' and even the highest concentrations are way below smoking levels.

★ It is no effort to obtain your nicotine from a cigarette − you just inhale the smoke and you receive your 'fix'. With nicotine gum it's rather tedious to have to keep chewing the gum to release the nicotine. You therefore have to work harder to get your nicotine and this is a very attractive safety feature of the gum. After 3 months of chewing nicotine gum you're rather fed up with this whole process of chewing and, therefore, long-term addiction is unlikely.

Therefore, do not worry about becoming addicted to the gum − this is not a common problem. But make sure you follow the exact instructions on how and when to stop using the gum.

WHAT STRENGTH OF GUM?

Nicorette is available in two strengths: 2mg and 4mg. To find out the strength that you will require to make stopping cigarettes more tolerable ask yourself these two questions:

Do you smoke more than 20 cigarettes per day?

Do you smoke your first cigarette of the day within twenty minutes of rising?

If you answer 'Yes' to both, you should use the 4mg gum (or two pieces of 2mg). Any other combination of answers implies that you should use the 2mg gum.

CHEWING TECHNIQUES

If you want to make the quit smoking process as easy as possible you will need to avoid as many of the unpleasant side-effects of the nicotine withdrawal syndrome as possible. To do this you must try to maintain a reasonable level of nicotine in your bloodstream throughout each day. Your first two weeks are a time when you should be chewing the nicotine gum as freely as possible. These are my tips:

★ Chew the gum very SLOWLY. This is not a confectionery gum, it is a medical treatment and you are in direct control of the rate of release of the drug into your own bloodstream. But you must control the release of nicotine by chewing slowly and that is not easy to do. The temptation will be to chew away at your own natural 'rate of chew', which will be too fast for correct Nicorette usage.

★ Continue to chew SLOWLY until you feel a strong taste developing in the mouth or at the back of the throat. This taste is due to the presence of nicotine in the mouth following release from the gum. This nicotine will now be absorbed through the lining of the mouth, to begin its journey through the bloodstream to the brain. Once the brain cells receive their nicotine, the craving to smoke is brought under control.

★ As soon as you are aware of the strong taste of nicotine, STOP chewing and allow the gum to rest in the corner of your mouth between your cheek and the inside of your gum. If you continue to chew the Nicorette instead of resting it, you will release more and more nicotine into your mouth and this high concentration, apart from its foul taste, may produce nausea, hiccups, indigestion and mouth ulcers. Releasing high concentrations of nicotine into the mouth will also reduce the level of nicotine going to the brain. This is because high doses of nicotine in the mouth will result in a lot of nicotine being swallowed and once nicotine is swallowed it never gets to the brain, as it is broken down by the liver into another substance called cotinine, which does not have the desired effects upon the brain.

★ It is difficult NOT to chew chewing gum when it's in your mouth, so do try and discipline yourself to rest it. Leave the gum 'parked', or resting, until the taste fades. Once the nicotine is absorbed through the lining of the inside of the mouth the taste fades. You must then start chewing the Nicorette gum again SLOWLY.

THE NICOTINE GUM 'CHEWING CYCLE'

To get the best effects from Nicorette, these four steps are easily remembered:

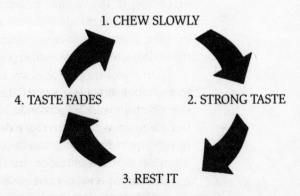

1. CHEW SLOWLY

2. STRONG TASTE

3. REST IT

4. TASTE FADES

Nicorette chewing cycle

By using the nicotine gum this way you are controlling the rate of release of nicotine into your mouth, so that not too much drug is released at once. If too much nicotine is released then it is swallowed with saliva down into the stomach. When swallowed, nicotine can cause excess acid in the stomach so if you are developing dyspepsia and heartburn you are probably chewing the gum too quickly. If you suffer from 'peptic' ulcers, either gastric or duodenal, then you should not use nicotine gum – but then, of course, neither should you be smoking!

For the first 3 to 4 days without cigarettes try and chew one piece of gum every hour, if possible on the hour every hour. You will then maintain a steady level of nicotine in your bloodstream, cushioning you against the severe cravings for a smoke that result from low blood nicotine levels.

After 3 to 4 days you can reduce your consumption to one piece of gum whenever you feel like a cigarette.

You are now using it only when necessary, but do not attempt to delay having your next piece of gum with the intention of rationing yourself to so many pieces per day. Any desire to smoke is, in effect, your brain crying out for nicotine – so chew the gum, and if one piece of gum does not remove the need to smoke, chew another piece immediately.

Many smokers go back to smoking by giving in to cigarettes when faced with unexpected stress. Over the years you have always had a cigarette when faced with stress and so you have developed a reflex to 'light up' when stress is upon you. This is a deeply ingrained response and an extremely difficult one to conquer. Unexpected stress is not easy to cope with if your blood nicotine levels are low, so chew the gum very freely during your first fortnight without cigarettes.

MY MUM HAS BEEN SMOKING SIXTY CIGARETTES A DAY FOR TEN YEARS. NOW SHE SAYS SHE'S DECIDED TO GIVE IT UP BEFORE IT BECOMES A HABIT.

THERE ARE ONLY TWO WAYS OF GIVING YOUR BRAIN THE NICOTINE IT CRAVES: FROM TOBACCO OR FROM NICOTINE PHASEOUT THERAPIES. TOBACCO KILLS – NICOTINE PHASEOUT THERAPIES DON'T!

After 30 to 45 minutes of chewing, the gum has released nearly all of its nicotine. From then on you are chewing 'blank' gum: no further nicotine is being released into your bloodstream.

If you are still troubled by the strong desire to smoke, then you need higher blood nicotine levels. The answer to this is to chew more gum. If you are chewing 15 or more pieces of 2mg gum daily then change up to the 4mg strength. In some countries only the 2mg strength is available. If this is the case then chew two pieces of the 2mg strength together each time you feel like a cigarette.

One piece of 4mg gum gives blood levels of nicotine equal to only half the level of that produced by one cigarette. So do be reassured that even if you were chewing 20 pieces of 4mg gum a day you would not be absorbing nicotine at dangerous levels: that would equate to only 10 cigarettes smoked — and how many cigarettes were you smoking before you gave up?

If you know that you are going to be faced with temptation from other smokers — for example by attending a party or some other social event — then prepare yourself beforehand so that you will not give in to the cigarettes offered to you. You do this by chewing more pieces of the nicotine gum in the 2 to 3 hours before you attend the function. Either chew two pieces at a time or chew single pieces more frequently, not forgetting that after 30 minutes of chewing the gum contains no more active nicotine. This manoeuvre will increase your blood nicotine level and decrease your desire to smoke even when faced with the greatest temptation of proffered cigarettes.

THIS IS A SITUATION WHERE PEOPLE WHO ARE TRYING TO STOP SMOKING OFTEN FAIL. SO TAKE MY ADVICE AND ANTICIPATE PROBLEM TIMES — CHEW MORE GUM TO PREVENT YOURSELF SMOKING.

And here's another tip learnt from my many years of experience:

NEVER LET YOUR SUPPLY OF NICOTINE PHASEOUT THERAPY, WHETHER GUM OR PATCHES, RUN TOO LOW.

If you run out of the gum you may well panic as you did when you ran out of cigarettes. You remember how you solved that problem? You rushed out and bought some cigarettes. There are plenty of cigarette vending machines around, but Nicorette gum can only be bought at your local pharmacy!

PROBLEMS WITH THE GUM

The two most common complaints are:

(1) It doesn't work.

(2) It tastes foul.

Here's how to deal with those problems:

IT DOESN'T WORK: In other words you're chewing the gum, and you're still dying for a cigarette! I have discovered several ways of helping you overcome this:

Chew faster. You might be chewing too slowly and not releasing enough nicotine for your own personal needs at that time. Every smoker is different. Some smokers need more nicotine than others. So you may have to ignore the 'chew slowly' advice given in the chewing cycle diagram if that 'rate of chew' is not controlling your desire to smoke.

Chew more. You may not be chewing enough pieces per day to control your personal withdrawal symptoms. If you're still dying for a smoke, you must chew more gum.

Chew four (4mg): You may need a higher dose of nicotine. At first, you will not know how much nicotine you need to control your own desire to smoke. If the 2mg strength is ineffective then change up to the 4mg gum.

IT TASTES FOUL: Some people find the taste of nicotine gum far too strong and feel unable to continue using it. This occurs more often with women smokers and with those who used to smoke the milder brands of cigarettes. Once again, I have a few tricks up my sleeve to help you through this problem.

Park it: If the taste is too unpleasant for you, then you may be very sensitive to oral nicotine. Slow the release of nicotine from the gum by resting it in the corner of your mouth and stop chewing. Treat Nicorette as a pastille or lozenge and just suck it from time to time. You don't have to chew it, for it to work.

Halve it: If one piece of the gum is too strong try halving it, then chewing half a piece at a time.

Mix it: To make the taste more acceptable, you could mix ordinary confectionery chewing gum with nicotine gum. Using Wrigleys Spearmint or any other flavour of gum will make the Nicorette more palatable and still effective at controlling your desire to smoke.

If you are extremely sensitive to the taste of the nicotine gum you could combine all of the above three solutions, in other words park it, halve it and mix it.

STOPPING
THE GUM

Use the gum for a minimum of 3 months. Do not try to reduce your consumption too early and do not stop it before you have reached the 3 month stage after quitting cigarettes. The gum is your own personal 'nicotine support system' whilst learning to live without your cigarettes. Do not try to manage without that support until you have done three months without cigarettes. If you are using the Smoker's Quit Chart at the back of this book, you will have marked your Quit Day for stopping smoking. On the chart you should now mark the day that falls exactly three months after your smoking Quit Day. This day is the day on which you start reducing your nicotine gum intake. And now here is another important tip based on a scientific understanding of the real meaning of nicotine addiction.

PLEASE DO **NOT** SUDDENLY STOP USING THE GUM, AS YOU DID WHEN YOU REPLACED CIGARETTES WITH GUM. GENTLY DOES IT!

You should gradually reduce your intake of the gum over a period of time, by following this recommended phaseout programme – indeed nothing could be simpler:

REDUCE BY ONE PIECE – EVERY WEEK.

For example, if at 3 months you were chewing 6 pieces of Nicorette daily, you would plan your phaseout programme, step by step, as follows:

First week:
Sunday to Saturday: 6 pieces every day.

Second week:
Sunday to Saturday: 5 pieces every day.

Third week:
Sunday to Saturday: 4 pieces every day.

Continue with this plan until your consumption reaches zero pieces per day. At this rate it would take you six weeks to phase out the gum, and there's no rush – remember you have been smoking for years and years.

Opposite are SOME ADDITIONAL USEFUL TIPS ON PHASING OUT THE GUM

★ If, for example, on one of those days you didn't use up your daily ration of 5 pieces, do not carry over any unused gum to the next day. The daily ration is the maximum number of pieces allowed on that day.

★ To help reduce your consumption of the gum, you might find it helpful to save the bulk of your daily ration until later in the day. Imagine the torment of having to survive from say 4.00pm with only 2 pieces of gum left for the rest of the day.

★ During your phaseout regime try chewing ordinary chewing gum in between your pieces of Nicorette. You may find chewing ordinary gum as helpful as using nicotine gum during the later stages. After three months of chewing you may find that you have almost become addicted to the chewing action rather than the nicotine in the gum.

★ Mark on your 'Smoker's Quit Chart' (see chapter headed 'Just For Today') the day that you stop using nicotine gum.

★ For the first few months after you have phased out the nicotine gum, make sure you still carry a few pieces of gum with you, just in case the old craving comes back or you are faced with temptation from other smokers. Better that you chew the odd piece of nicotine gum than light up a cigarette!

★ You are now off the gum and you have gone 3 months without a cigarette.

CONGRATULATIONS YOU'VE MADE IT!

QUITTERS' STORIES

Mrs. F.G., designer . . .

"I had put off using nicotine gum for about 18 months because I thought it might cause mouth cancer. When I realised that tar caused the cancer and not nicotine, I gave the gum a try and I stopped smoking! It was easy, I couldn't believe it!"

Mr. C.D., journalist . . .

"They even gave me some Nicorette, which is in fact, nicotine-containing chewing gum. Every time I feel like a smoke, I have a chew and the craving goes."

Mrs. M.M., administrator . . .

"I don't like chewing gum. So I followed the advice to regard it as a pastille or lozenge, and so I didn't chew it – I just let it sit in the corner of my mouth, and I still got nicotine from it. I wasn't keen on the idea of using a chewing gum containing an addictive drug! I thought, 'My God, what next? Heroin chewing gum?' Well I tried it and I was amazed at how easy it was for me to stop smoking, and how easy it was to get off the gum.

"I had tried every stop-smoking treatment previously available, but with nicotine gum it was far easier to quit smoking than with any other method I had used. Whenever I saw a 'No Smoking' sign, I'd pop in my nicotine gum and smile, knowing that I would be getting my nicotine whilst those poor smokers were craving for theirs."

TOBACCO TRIVIA

Here is a selection of 'Tobacco Trivia' questions to test your knowledge, and, hopefully, to keep you in a light-hearted mood as you while away your smoke-free hours!

QUESTIONS:

1. Children of parents who smoke are 7 times more likely to smoke than children whose parents don't. True or false?

2. Do women who smoke tend to reach the menopause earlier or later than average?

3. Which is the 'Safe' cigarette?
a. Filter tip   b. Low tar   c. No filter
d. One that hasn't been lit

4. Which historical figure popularised smoking in England?

5. Tobacco was America's first cash crop. True or false?

6. What percentage of people with chronic bronchitis are smokers?

7. Most ex-smokers gain weight. True or false?

8. What percentage of the population are ex-smokers?

9. How quickly will the body begin to repair itself after someone stops smoking?
a. 1 hour   b. 12 hours
c. 6 months   d. 12 months

10. Cigarette smoking is one of the three major causes of heart attack and blood vessel disease. What are the other two?

11. At the turn of the century the annual death rate for lung cancer was 10 deaths per 100,000 males. What was the figure in the 1980s?

12. George Washington grew tobacco. True or false?

13. Virtually all patients with cancer of the throat are smokers. True or false?

14. How many years of life will a smoker lose, on average?

15. What is "Passive Smoking"?

16. What percentage of smokers have seriously tried to stop smoking and failed?

17. After which war were cigarettes manufactured for the first time?

18. Carbon monoxide is present in high concentration in cigarette smoke. True or false?

ANSWERS:

1. True. 2. Earlier. 3. The Unlit One! 4. Sir Walter Raleigh (1552 – 1618). 5. True. 6. 95%. 7. False (about 40% gain weight). 8. 25%. Between 10 – 11 million adults have managed to give up, so you could join them! 9. 12 hours. Within 12 hours of smoking your last cigarette the immediate effects of the toxic substances will begin to lessen. Constricted blood vessels return to normal; blood pressure and heart rate decrease; your lungs should clear of noxious gases and be able to work more efficiently; muscle tremor should also decrease. 10. High blood pressure and high cholesterol level. 11. 200 deaths per 100,000 males. 12. True, as did Sir Walter Raleigh. 13. True. 14. 10 to 15 years. 15. The inhalation by non-smokers of other people's smoke. 16. 70%. 17. The Crimean War (1853 – 1856). 18. True.

Chapter 9

Through the Skin: Nicotine Skin Patch Replacement Therapy

A RECIPE FOR SUCCESS

More successful than any previous treatment to help smokers, the nicotine replacement skin patches have in several studies doubled, or even quadrupled, the smoker's chances of quitting. These therapies will work best as part of a planned programme of quitting and this is why I have incorporated them into my TEN POINT QUIT PLAN. As a smoker, you can feel very alone when you are trying to quit. And you will have already gathered from the previous chapters that there is more to the process of quitting than just sticking a nicotine replacement patch onto your skin and hoping for the best. I hope that in reading this book you do not feel alone – and that you have a friend in there with you.

So let's have a look at how you can incorporate the very successful nicotine skin patches into the overall NICOTINE PHASEOUT PROGRAMME to get you off your cigarettes.

YOUR FIRST PATCH

Before you start your Nicotine Reduction Therapy, I just want to check that you are making full use of the very helpful supporting techniques I explained in the earlier chapters –

★ firstly, that you have already decided upon the actual date of your Quit Day.

★ secondly, that you have tried to get a friend, partner or work colleague to quit with you.

★ and finally, that you've prepared your 'CASH NOT ASH' jar.

I have designed these techniques especially for you after 15 years of intensive experience in helping many thousands of people quit smoking.

APPLYING THE PATCH

The patch should be applied to an area of dry skin that is relatively free of hair. The middle outer part of your upper arm and the inner aspect of the lower arm are both suitable areas, as may be your hip, leg, chest or, and perhaps especially, your bottom. The site is not critical. It's your body – stick it where you like!

Hold the patch firmly in position and **count slowly** up to 10, thereby allowing the pressure-sensitive adhesive to stick firmly to the skin. It should remain well stuck down even during showering, swimming or bathing.

The patch will stick poorly if you have any body spray, perfume or deodorant on the skin where the patch is to be placed. This is particularly so if you apply it after you have had a bath or shower, when you will need to dry your skin thoroughly and then allow time for your skin temperature to cool down before applying a new patch.

The timing of the first patch application is crucial. In the case of Nicotinell, it should NOT be applied on the morning of the Quit Day, since that will be too late. You should apply your first patch just before bedtime on your LAST day of smoking, just after finishing your very last cigarette.

In the case of Nicabate or Nicorette, you should apply your first patch as soon as you wake up on your designated Quit Day. I suggest that my patients who choose the morning patches should smoke their last cigarette soon after waking on the Quit Day. Although the manufacturers do not recommend this, I have found it useful in preventing the craving during the first hour or two while the patch is beginning to take effect.

---

24 HOUR VERSUS 16 HOUR PATCHES?

Clearly there are some differences between the patches made by different manufacturers and probably the biggest difference is in the length of time you are expected to wear them on your skin.

With 24-hour patches, the nicotine released into the skin throughout the night is intended to ease cravings and withdrawal the following morning. With the 16-hour patch, the intention is only to cover you during the waking hours, on the basis that you do not smoke while asleep so you do not need the extra nicotine during the sleeping hours. There are clearly pros and cons for either philosophy.

You are probably dreading that day ... your Quit Day morning ... when you expect to feel that immediate and desperate longing for a cigarette! With your 24-hour patch already applied the night before, it may be an additional comfort to know that wearing the patch might make it a little easier to cope with first thing in the morning.

On the other hand, with the 16-hour patch, disturbed sleep is said to be less common in the first few weeks on patch therapy.

At present, there appear to be no studies comparing the effectiveness of the 16-hour patch with the 24-hour patch over long periods of time, so that the selection of which patch to use is up to you — "You pays your money, and you takes your choice!"

At the expiry of the patch, whether first thing in the morning or last thing at night, the patch should be removed. In the case of the 24-hour type you apply a new patch immediately; in the case of the 16-hour type, you remain patch-free during sleep and the fresh patch is applied first thing after waking. Fold the old patch over on itself and discard it in the rubbish bin, well away from children, as it will still contain some residual nicotine.

ARE YOU WORRIED ABOUT CRAVINGS OR WITHDRAWAL SYMPTOMS AFTER THE PATCH?

I am delighted to be able to assure you that there are rarely any withdrawal problems when the last course of treatment is completed. Remember that you have been gradually weaning yourself off your nicotine over quite a long period of time — 12 weeks. Those 12 weeks were the most critical time for you as a 'quitter', because it has been found that more than 75 per cent of all relapses back to smoking happen during the first 3 months of quitting. The most intense withdrawal symptoms are known to occur during the first 4 weeks and then they gradually subside over the course of the next 4 weeks.

WORRIED ABOUT WEIGHT GAIN?

If you are a bit frightened about putting on weight and this is making you wary of considering the skin patch therapy, I have good news for you. I am delighted to say that research has shown that weight gain is rarely a problem in people giving up smoking using the nicotine skin patches. As has been pointed out already, patients who used the nicotine patch daily for 3 months only put on a few ounces in weight, whereas those patients who were given a 'blank' patch containing no nicotine put on 9.7lbs during that first 3 months! It seems that the nicotine in the patch does really help to prevent that weight gain.

ARE THERE ANY SIDE-EFFECTS OR CONTRA-INDICATIONS TO THE USE OF SKIN PATCHES?

In the following chapter, I discuss the relatively minor unwanted effects of nicotine replacement therapy and compare these with the very serious unwanted effects of smoking.

Nicotine replacement skin patches are not recommended for use by non-smokers, children, pregnant women or mothers who are breast feeding. Nor should they be used by patients who have a known hypersensitivity reaction to nicotine, or the other constituents of skin plasters.

DOES THE BRAND OR STRENGTH OF CIGARETTE MATTER?

No. As explained in an earlier chapter, people adjust the number of cigarettes they smoke, regardless of brand or strength, to obtain the desired blood levels of nicotine. This should make no difference to the dose of nicotine patch therapy.

YOU SHOULD NOT SMOKE WHILST WEARING THE PATCHES

Patients with heart disease, high blood pressure, peptic ulcers, circulation problems, over-active thyroid and diabetes should discuss their request for nicotine patches with their doctor before commencing treatment.

Although this is not mandatory and the treatments are all available to you from your local pharmacy, I would, as a general guide, recommend that you have a word with your doctor before starting any nicotine replacement therapy. Your doctor could certainly advise you on the above precautions and most doctors are very committed to helping their patients give up smoking.

DETAILS OF THE INDIVIDUAL PATCHES

There are three patches you should now consider: Nicabate, Nicotinell and Nicorette. A fourth patch, Niconil, is not yet available in the UK but may become available later this year. I shall describe each in some detail and you will find a helpful address or telephone number for each of the patches in the list at the back of this book. For further details, see the manufacturer's instructions with each specific patch.

NICABATE

Nicabate is a 24-hour nicotine replacement skin patch manufactured by the American pharmaceutical company, Marion Merrell Dow. This patch is not currently 'blacklisted' so it can be prescribed on the NHS, but this situation will probably change in the near future.

Nicabate can be bought over the counter at your local pharmacy without any prescription. This makes it more accessible to the smoker, as no visit to the doctor is needed. Nicabate can also be obtained on private prescription, which makes it cheaper than buying it direct from the pharmacist, as no VAT is charged if you are buying it with a private prescription.

Obviously the cheapest way to obtain this patch is on a NHS prescription, but this will finally depend upon your family doctor's attitude with regard to smoking being treatable on the NHS.

Nicabate comes in three strengths:

Nicabate 21 – delivering 21mg of nicotine.

Nicabate 14 – delivering 14mg of nicotine.

Nicabate 7 – delivering 7mg of nicotine.

NICABATE
DOSAGE
ROUTINE

For smokers of 10 or more cigarettes per day the recommended dosage routine is as follows:

Nicabate 21 – daily for the first 6 weeks.

Nicabate 14 – daily for the next 2 weeks.

Nicabate 7 – daily for the last 2 weeks.

This 6 weeks, 2 weeks and 2 weeks regime is called the 'Nicabate 6-2-2 system', which is a method of weaning the smoker off his nicotine by reducing the patch size and nicotine content over a 10-week period.

If necessary Nicabate may be used for a further 6 weeks. Smokers who have heart problems, who weigh less than 7 stones, or who smoke less than 10 cigarettes per day, should start on the middle strength patch 'Nicabate 14' for the first 6 weeks and then use the 'Nicabate 7' for the final 4 weeks.

These patches come in 7 and 14-day pack sizes and the carton is a 'flip top' packet, similar to a cigarette packet.

APPLYING THE PATCH

Since Nicabate is a 24-hour patch, you should apply the first patch AFTER FINISHING YOUR LAST CIGARETTE on the morning of your Quit Day. Some people may, however, prefer to apply the patch at bedtime to remove any craving for nicotine immediately after waking. Choose your area of skin as advised above and hold the patch firmly in position for 10 seconds. The Nicabate Patch works more quickly than other patches, as it contains nicotine in the actual adhesive of the sticking plaster, so that as soon as it is applied some nicotine starts getting absorbed into the skin to quickly control the withdrawal cravings.

The patch also uses a special type of drug delivery technology, where a thin membrane separates the reservoir of nicotine from the skin. This membrane is called a rate-controlling membrane, and is not found in the other nicotine skin patches. The membrane controls the actual rate of release from the patch into the skin, with the aim of maintaining a steady concentration in the bloodstream. Skin reactions tend to be less troublesome with this patch as a result of its rate-controlling membrane. Nevertheless, when a new patch is applied, it should be put on a different area of skin, to avoid possible skin reactions.

This patch is intended to be used throughout 24 hours. It is worn through the night and the following day. In the evening, it is removed, folded over on itself and safely discarded; then the next patch is applied.

If a patch is removed and no further patch is applied, very little nicotine can be detected in the blood after 12 hours.

UNWANTED EFFECTS OF NICABATE

This is a very safe treatment. However, the precautions listed in the introduction to this chapter apply to Nicabate, as they do to all nicotine patch therapies. Because Nicabate delivers nicotine into the body for a 24-hour period, sleep disturbance can occur. Sleep disturbance of this type is, however, known to occur with stopping smoking even without nicotine replacement therapy, and these effects usually wear off after the second week.

THE NICABATE POSTAL SUPPORT PROGRAMME

When you get your prescription from the doctor or the patch from your chemist, you should receive an enrolment card, with a Freephone telephone number to ring. When you call that number quote your name, address, Quit Date and personal enrolment number (on front of enrolment card). Then within 2 to 3 days you will receive a package through the post, which is the first of 4 items that will be sent to you free of charge as part of the Postal Support Programme:

At 2 to 3 days:

Package 1 arrives – this contains a letter, support leaflets, and a 70-day wall-chart on which you record your progress over the 10-week treatment period. A diary card, badge, no-smoking stickers and a relaxation tape are also included.

At 10 days:

Package 2 arrives – this contains a letter and support leaflet giving tips against temptation.

At Week 5½:

Package 3 arrives – this contains a letter, more support leaflets dealing with weight control and cash savings, and a reply paid card to request your non-smoker certificate – provided you have successfully stopped smoking. You should be honest!

At Week 10:

Package 4 arrives – this contains a final letter and a Non-Smoker Certificate of Achievement.

Package 1 is a red box, and the other packages are in red envelopes, to highlight your red-letter days.

NICOTINELL TTS

Nicotinell TTS is another 24-hour skin patch as described above. It is manufactured by a Swiss pharmaceutical company – Ciba Geigy.

Apply the first patch last thing at night. Subsequent patches can be applied at night or first thing in the morning, according to preference.

Nicotinell is available in three sizes – 'Nicotinell 30', 'Nicotinell 20' and 'Nicotinell 10'. Each delivers a different dose of nicotine over a 24-hour period.

Nicotinell 30 delivers approximately 21mg of nicotine.

Nicotinell 20 delivers approximately 14mg of nicotine.

Nicotinell 10 delivers approximately 7mg of nicotine.

Do note that the number at the end of the patch name – for example Nicotinell 30 – relates to the size of the patch and not the concentration of nicotine in the patch. Smokers of 20 or more cigarettes a day should follow this dosage routine:

1st month – Nicotinell 30, one patch daily for 4 weeks.

2nd month – Nicotinell 20, one patch daily for 4 weeks.

3rd month – Nicotinell 10, one patch daily for 4 weeks.

4th month – end of treatment, no more patches needed.

Smokers using less than 20 cigarettes per day are advised to use Nicotinell 20 for month one and two, and then Nicotinell 10 for the third month.

The basic plan with this type of treatment is that the smoker undergoes a 'step by step' reduction in his or her nicotine intake over a period of 12 weeks.

Each patch is available in two pack sizes:

1. One week's supply of 7 patches.

2. One month's supply of 28 patches.

The cost of the patch is equivalent to the cost of a similar supply of cigarettes, in other words the 7-day pack costs about the same as one week's cigarettes and the 28-day pack the same as one month's supply of cigarettes.

All three strengths, Nicotinell 30, 20 and 10, are available as 7-day and 28-day packs.

Whichever strength you start with, make sure that your first pack is called a Patient Help Pack, because this first pack contains a lot of support materials that you will find useful during the early days of quitting.

PHASING OUT NICOTINE USING NICOTINELL

Before the end of the first month of quitting, you should see your doctor or pharmacist for your second month's supply of Nicotinell. At this point you will change down to the Nicotinell 20 patch and use that every day for the second month of treatment.

At the end of this second month, you will then change down to the final treatment pack – Nicotinell 10, which is worn daily for another 28 days, when the course of treatment comes to an end.

UNWANTED
EFFECTS OF
NICOTINELL
SKIN PATCH

On the whole this is a very safe treatment but the general precautions listed above apply. You should read the whole of this chapter through carefully. As a 24-hour patch, there is a slight tendency to sleep disturbance which is at its worst in the first two weeks or so. Sleep disturbance is of course a common feature of stopping smoking even without nicotine replacement therapy and it usually clears up after the first 2 weeks.

SMOKER'S
SUPPORT
PACK

Along with the Nicotinell 30 patches, you will receive a SMOKER'S SUPPORT PACK, which includes a booklet of practical tips on how to cope without cigarettes, and an emergency card to help you deal with moments of temptation.

Further help is also available from the manufacturer's 'STUB OUT AND STAY FREE' offer – see manufacturer's SMOKEFREE HELPLINE number at the back of this book.

NICORETTE PATCH

Manufactured by the same company that produces the 'Nicorette Gum' – a Swedish company called Kabi Pharmacia – Nicorette is the only 16-hour patch available at present. Meant to be worn only during the waking hours and taken off during sleep, it is known as the 'daytime patch'.

WHY A DAYTIME ONLY PATCH?

The pros and cons of 16-hour versus 24-hour patches were discussed earlier in this chapter. It has been found that a small percentage of smokers who use the 24-hour patches do complain of sleep disturbance. However, sleep disturbance is a common complication of stopping smoking even without nicotine replacement and usually these night-time problems wear off after a couple of weeks on the 24-hour patches.

If you use Nicorette, you receive nicotine continuously through the skin throughout the waking hours, but then the patch is taken off at bedtime. Blood nicotine levels then fall during sleep and the smoker puts on a new patch the next morning. Advocates of the 24-hour patches would claim that this takes about 1 to 2 hours to deliver nicotine into the blood stream, creating a vulnerable period first thing after waking. But in fact experience with this patch has shown it to be very successful.

The Nicorette Patch can be bought over the counter in your local pharmacy without any prescription. It is also available on private prescription, when you can save yourself the VAT because private prescriptions are exempt from VAT.

The Nicorette Patch comes in three strengths:

Nicorette Patch 15mg, delivering 15mg over 16 hours.

Nicorette Patch 10mg, delivering 10mg over 16 hours.

Nicorette Patch 5mg, delivering 5mg over 16 hours.

USING THE NICORETTE PATCH

Unlike the other two patches that are worn for 24 hours, and applied before bedtime, the Nicorette Patch has to be applied in the morning, worn throughout the day and taken off at bedtime. So the first patch should be applied immediately after awakening at the start of your Quit Day.

UNWANTED EFFECTS OF THE NICORETTE PATCH

This is a very safe type of treatment. However, the general precautions described above apply, as they do to all patches. Before opting for any kind of patch therapy, you should read this chapter through carefully. Because you have been without nicotine during sleep and because this is your first day – your most important day in the quitting programme – I allow my patients on Nicorette to have one last cigarette after getting up on the morning of their Quit Day! So your Quit Day will actually start with one cigarette – your last cigarette, which will pump some nicotine quickly into your bloodstream to 'get you up and going'. I should, however, add that the manufacturers of Nicorette think this final cigarette unnecessary. The choice, once again, is up to you.

APPLYING THE PATCH

As soon as you get up on your Quit Day, you should apply your first Nicorette Patch, which will supply you with nicotine throughout the rest of the day. Press the patch onto your skin, following the manufacturer's instructions, and hold it in position, whilst you count up to 10. The patch will then stay in position, even whilst bathing or swimming.

Before going to bed, you must remove the Nicorette Patch and dispose of it safely. Do not wear any Nicorette Patch during the night, but put your fresh one on first thing the next morning.

PHASING OUT NICOTINE USING NICORETTE PATCH

It is recommended that the Nicorette Patch should be used over 12 weeks in a 'step down' pattern so that you are gradually weaned off the nicotine. Smokers, or should I say ex-smokers, should follow this dosage routine:

First 8 weeks – use Nicorette Patch 15mg for 16hrs/day.

Next 2 weeks – use Nicorette Patch 10mg for 16hrs/day.

Last 2 weeks – use Nicorette Patch 5mg for 16hrs/day.

This dosage regime applies to all ex-smokers, no matter what your previous cigarette consumption.

Nicorette Patch is available in 7-day and 28-day packs. The manufacturers advise you not to wear two patches at a time or to smoke whilst wearing the patch.

THE 'FRESH START' SUPPORT PACK

A patient support programme is also available, either from your pharmacist, GP or practice nurse. The package is called the 'FRESH START' support pack and includes a booklet on how to give up smoking successfully. There is also a Smoker's Quitline, called 'FRESH START'.

If you would like initial advice on Nicorette or help after you have started it, the 'Nicorette Help-desk' number is given at the end of this book.

TOBACCO TRIVIA

Here is a selection of 'Tobacco Trivia' questions to test your knowledge, and hopefully, to keep you in a light-hearted mood, whilst you while away your smoke-free hours!

QUESTIONS:

1. Which professional group has the lowest incidence of cigarette smoking?

2. How many different substances and chemicals are to be found in tobacco?
a. 4,000   b. 800   c. 300

3. When was cigarette advertising banned on British television?

4. Do smokers who switch from cigarettes to pipes or cigars reduce the risk of heart attack?

5. Who wrote. . ."Stopping smoking is easy. I ought to know because I've done it a thousand times"?

6. A 55-year-old smoker will have taken how many shots of nicotine since he started smoking?
a. 200,000   b. 1,500,000   c. 3,500,000

7. What is the most important requirement when trying to stop smoking?

8. How much money do the under-16s spend on cigarettes each year?
a. £60 million   b. £30 million
c. £40 million

ANSWERS: 1. Doctors. 2. 4,000. This includes nicotine, tar, carbon monoxide, hydrogen cyanide, ammonia, acetone, and even arsenic. Over 40 of these chemicals are known to cause cancer. 3. 1966. 4. No, the risk may be increased, as they inhale the cigar or pipe smoke which is much stronger than cigarette smoke. Pipe and cigar smokers don't usually inhale. 5. Mark Twain. 6. 3,500,000 shots. 7. A real determination to stop and stay stopped! 8. £60 million. It is illegal to sell cigarettes to children under the age of 16 years!

COMPLETING THE COURSE OF NICOTINE PATCH THERAPY

The usual course of patch replacement therapy will last about 3 months.

FINALLY THE LAST PATCH IS REMOVED AND YOU HAVE SUCCESSFULLY PHASED NICOTINE OUT OF YOUR LIFE!

CONGRATULATIONS – YOU'VE MADE IT!

Chapter 10

It's Enough To Make You Sick

ARE THERE
SIDE-EFFECTS
OF NICOTINE
SKIN PATCH
THERAPY?

Some people have a perfectly understandable worry that using any kind of medication, such as the nicotine patch therapy, might have unwanted effects. Are there, for example, people who should not use the patches? What side-effects might you expect if you use them? Most important of all, how do any such unwanted effects compare with the unwanted effects of continuing to smoke?

First, let me reassure you that there are very few disadvantages of wearing the nicotine skin patches. As a general rule I would recommend that you talk to your family doctor if you are at all worried about potential side-effects or if you think the contra-indications might apply to you. Remember that your doctor is your friend in this: the majority of doctors are very committed to helping their patients stop smoking. First of all, let me repeat the contra-indications from the previous chapter.

CONTRA-
INDICATIONS
TO SKIN
PATCHES

Nicotine replacement skin patches are not recommended for use by non-smokers, children, pregnant women or mothers who are breast feeding. Nor should they be used by patients who have a known hypersensitivity to nicotine or to the other constituents of skin plasters.

PEOPLE WHO SHOULD BE CAUTIOUS AND TAKE THEIR DOCTOR'S ADVICE

Patients with heart disease, high blood pressure, peptic ulcers, circulation problems, an over-active thyroid or diabetes should discuss their wish to use nicotine patches with their family doctor before commencing treatment.

SOME USEFUL GENERAL GUIDANCE

★ Firstly, and as a sensible general precaution, if you think you are suffering a reaction, report this to your doctor and take his or her advice.

★ Skin irritation – this is not a common effect. However, nicotine can irritate the skin in some people. If you notice any reddening or itchiness of the skin after removing the patch, ensure that you put your fresh patch on a different part of the body. This is to be recommended as a routine anyway for all nicotine patch wearers. Keep changing the site of application, even if you don't suffer any skin reaction.

★ Sleep disturbance – a small percentage of users of the 24 hour patches, Nicotinell and Nicabate, have reported certain sleep problems. Dreams, nightmares and poor sleeping are the most common problems. Such complaints arise anyhow when you stop smoking without using any nicotine treatment, but there does seem to be a slight increase in the problems when the patch is worn through the night. For most patients

113

these sleep problems are not too irksome and for many they disappear after the first 10 to 14 days.

IT'S ENOUGH TO MAKE YOU SICK – VERY SICK!

To be absolutely objective, we have looked in detail at potential unwanted effects of nicotine replacement patch therapy. Now let's take a similarly objective look at the alternative, the unwanted effects of continuing to smoke cigarettes!

THESE ARE WHAT TOBACCO SMOKE CONTAINS

Carcinogens

Carcinogens are cancer-causing agents. The main culprits in tobacco smoke – and we all know that tobacco smoke carries a very high risk of causing lung cancer and many other types of cancer – are chemical substances known as polycyclic aromatic hydrocarbons, and N-nitroso compounds.

Intake of N-nitrosamines into the body in food or drink is strictly controlled by government regulations. The upper limit allowed in food or drink is **1 part per billion.** The concentration of N-nitrosamines in tobacco smoke is **2,000-9,000 parts per billion!** Yet there are no government regulations to control this source of powerful, cancer-causing agents.

Carbon monoxide

The gas carbon monoxide is colourless, odourless, tasteless and deadly. It dissolves in the blood 200 times faster than oxygen. In heavy smokers (20 or more per day), as much as 15 per cent of their haemoglobin is converted to carboxyhaemoglobin which is then unavailable to carry oxygen. This has very important implications for those smokers suffering from conditions of poor circulation or poor blood supply to organs such as the brain, heart or the legs.

In industry, Government regulations forbid exposure to carbon monoxide levels over **50 parts per million.** Tobacco smoke concentrations range from **1,000-50,000 parts per million.**

Irritants

Over 3,000 irritant substances have been identified in cigarettes. These chemicals cause narrowing of the airways and paralysis of the cilia, which are little hair-like cells that 'brush' particles of dirt, tar or any other foreign substances up the airways for us to cough up and expel from the lungs. Paralysis of these cilia causes increased contact time with the carcinogens from the tobacco smoke.

The irritant action of these chemicals causes other cells, called goblet cells, to produce more mucus, which stagnates as a result of the cilia being paralysed. The smaller airway tubes then become blocked and infected. The thin walls of the air sacs deep inside the lungs are eroded by these powerful chemicals, and this destruction of vital lung tissue results in a condition called emphysema, which causes such severe shortage of breath that even getting dressed makes the patient gasp for air. He or she may then have to carry oxygen around throughout the day, as simple tasks such as having a shave or a wash result in the patient fighting for breath.

Nicotine – or In the Nick O'Time!

Nicotine is an alkaloid drug, found mainly in the tobacco plant. It is highly addictive and has some very interesting drug-like effects in the body.

After sleeping all night the smoker's blood nicotine level is very low. If the smoker does not 'light up' within an hour or so of awakening, she or he feels irritable, anxious, aggressive and cannot concentrate. A cigarette quickly clears these uncomfortable symptoms, and it's the nicotine that is responsible for the rapid relief – not the carbon monoxide, tar or irritant substances.

Nicotine from a cigarette is detectable in the brain cells within 7 seconds of inhaling. An intravenous injection would take 14 seconds to produce the same effect!

You will remember from earlier in this book that nicotine in small doses acts as a stimulant, whilst in larger doses it becomes an effective tranquilliser. Smokers will, unknowingly, adjust their inhalation rate to produce the necessary effects they need, depending upon their environment and circumstances. Just watch how a smoker under stress inhales strongly, deeply and quickly from a cigarette, whilst a bored smoker 'passing the time of day' will just puff lightly, slowly and not inhale deeply.

WHAT'S
YOUR
POISON?

These are just a small selection of what you get when you inhale tobacco smoke:

Acetone (paint stripper).
Hydrogen cyanide (poison used in gas chambers).
Methanol (rocket fuel).

Ammonia (floor cleaner).

Toluene (industrial solvent).

Arsenic (powerful poison).

Dimethylnitrosamine (cancer provoking).

Phenol (poisonous solvent).

Napthalene (mothballs).

Butane (lighter fuel).

Cadmium (component in car battery).

DDT (insecticide).

Carbon monoxide (poisonous gas in car exhausts).

I haven't even listed a host of complex chemicals which are known to have powerful cancer-provoking properties, exposure to which is absolutely forbidden by the Health And Safety Regulations concerning the workplace.

A LIST OF SMOKING-RELATED DISEASES

A glance at this list will make you realise why I, as a family doctor, have devoted my life to helping smokers. Smoking is not the only cause of these conditions but it is a very important contributor.

★ Cancers of: mouth, larynx (voice box), oesophagus (gullet), breast, bronchus (windpipe), pancreas (gland producing insulin and digestive juices), kidney, bladder, cervix.

★ Heart attack.

★ Angina − poor blood supply to the heart.

★ Hypertension − high blood pressure.

★ Aortic aneurysm − tearing of main blood vessel from the heart.

117

★ Subarachnoid haemorrhage − brain haemorrhage.

★ Peripheral limb ischaemia − gangrene of feet and legs.

★ Cerebral ischaemia − poor blood supply to brain.

★ Strokes, which cause paralysis and death.

★ Chronic obstructive airways disease − bronchitis and emphysema.

★ Peptic ulcers of the stomach and duodenum.

★ Oesophageal reflux − heartburn.

★ Impotence − loss of penile erection.

★ A type of blindness − tobacco amblyopia.

THE LINK
BETWEN
SMOKING,
PREGNANCY
AND
CHILDREN

In pregnancy, smoking mums are more prone to the following problems:

★ Miscarriage.

★ Intra-uterine growth retardation – immature baby.

★ Hypertension of pregnancy – pre-eclampsia.

★ Premature labour.

★ Stillbirth.

★ Abnormalities affecting the unborn baby.

★ An increased risk of the baby's death within first few weeks of life.

THE
CHILDREN
OF SMOKING
PARENTS ARE
MORE PRONE
TO

★ Becoming smokers themselves.

★ Glue ear – causes deafness.

★ Colds.

★ Chest infections and meningitis.

★ Bronchiolitis/bronchitis.

★ Asthma.

★ Leukaemia and Hodgkin's disease.

SMOKERS –
YOU'RE
GETTING A
RAW DEAL!

Did you know that after the launch, in the UK, of the skin patch Nicotinell, you could have obtained this treatment on NHS prescription? Well at least for the first few months, until it was 'blacklisted' on 2 November 1992 by the Department of Health. Once a drug is blacklisted, a GP cannot isssue it on an NHS prescription, as the NHS will not pay for it – then the patient has to get a private prescription from their GP to allow them to buy the treatment themselves.

Before it was 'blacklisted', some smokers were lucky, in that their GPs believed that this treatment should be available on the NHS and they did issue NHS prescriptions for Nicotinell patches.

I belong to that group of GPs, because if I, and **every** GP in the country, can offer NHS prescriptions to treat **every other** type of addiction, such as alcoholism and heroin addiction, then we should at least be able to do the very same for smokers who are addicted to tobacco. What is very wrong is that you as a smoker have been discriminated against within the NHS, and as a result you have to pay for the treatment for your addiction.

ADDICTIONS, MURDERS, AIDS and SMOKING

Smoking kills more people per year than heroin addiction, alcohol, cocaine, crack, suicide, murders, fires, car accidents and AIDS, **all combined together!**

Current smoking-related deaths run at about 300 per day – which is equivalent to a fully laden Jumbo Jet crashing every other day of the year, and all passengers on board being killed. Can you imagine the hue and cry that would follow such headlines as:

4th March

JUMBO JET CRASHES AT HEATHROW – NO SURVIVORS!

6th March

JUMBO CRASHES AT RINGWAY – ALL DEAD!

Obviously, the Government would promptly intervene to find out the reason for such carnage and death, and you can see the headlines...

7th March

GOVERNMENT GROUNDS ALL JUMBOS!

But do you see anything being done actively to curtail the carnage and death being caused by smoking? Of course you don't, because, although treating those unfortunate patients who develop smoking-related diseases costs the NHS £1.5 million each day, the income from tobacco tax to the Government is **£17.2 million each day!**

So the Government, whilst claiming to be committed to reducing smoking levels by the year 2000, is making a net profit of **£15.7 million every single day** from cigarette smokers.

330 CIGARETTE SMOKERS DIE IN THE UK EVERY DAY! EVERY DAY THE UK GOVERNMENT COLLECTS £15.7 MILLION FROM CIGARETTE SMOKERS!

The message would appear to be:

SMOKERS – KEEP SMOKING. YOUR GOVERNMENT NEEDS YOU!

Now wouldn't you think that a Government might just be concerned enough to offer some help to those people who as a result of their addiction to tobacco stand a much reduced chance of enjoying their retirement? After all, 40 per cent of smokers do not live to collect their pension.

What you should be concerned about as a smoker and an NHS patient is that **you** are the **only** patient with a recognised addiction who cannot receive treatment for that addiction on the NHS. Yet the Government and Department of Health has the stated objective of tackling the problem of smoking in the coming years. Indeed it has committed itself to achieving certain targets by the year 2000, as highlighted in its own White Paper –

THE HEALTH OF THE NATION – WHITE PAPER, JULY 1992.

In the end, the decision of whether or not to smoke is a matter of individual choice, although this is influenced by many factors, not least – for those who already smoke – the fact that nicotine is addictive.

This paper contains some impressive targets and ideals. But how is it going to achieve these when it doesn't even allow GPs to prescribe effective stop-smoking treatments, like nicotine gum and nicotine skin patches, on the NHS for their addicted smokers?

STAYING STOPPED:

From the politics, I want to take you back to the task in hand...

HOPEFULLY YOU HAVE NOW MANAGED TO STOP SMOKING USING THE NICOTINE PHASEOUT PROGRAMME. HOW CAN YOU MAKE SURE THAT YOU STAY STOPPED?

TOBACCO TRIVIA

Here is a selection of 'Tobacco Trivia' questions to test your knowledge, and hopefully, to keep you in a light-hearted mood, as you while away your smoke-free hours!

QUESTIONS:

1. Women who smoke and take the oral contraceptive pill are twenty times more likely to have a heart attack or stroke than non-smokers on the pill. True or false!

2. How many trees are cut down to produce an acre of tobacco?
a. 50   b. 120   c. 150

3. What other plants belong to the same family as the tobacco plant?

4. If you smoked 20 cigarettes a day, how much could you save in one month if you gave up?
a. £67.02   b. £48.91   c. £52.75

5. Smokers are more prone to duodenal ulcers than non-smokers. True or false?

6. The number of males smoking has decreased in recent years. True or false?

7. The number of females smoking has decreased in recent years. True or false?

8. Smoking is given as the cause of 80% of all deaths from which of the following diseases?
a. Chronic bronchitis   b. Emphysema
c. Heart disease   d. Lung cancer

9. What percentage of smokers will die prematurely because of their smoking?

10. Which countries are the major producers of tobacco?

ANSWERS:

1. True. 2. 150. The 20 per day smoker is therefore responsible for the death of one tree every fortnight. 3. Potato, tomato and aubergine. 4. £67.02 (with cigarettes at £2.23 for twenty). That's equal to £804.44 a year. It's also equivalent to giving yourself a pay rise of £89.33 per month or £1072 per year before tax. 5. True. 6. True. 7. False. The prevalence of smoking amongst females has increased, especially amongst girls. 8. Chronic bronchitis, emphysema and lung cancer. And smoking is to blame for up to 25% of coronary heart disease deaths. 9. About 33%. 10. USA, China, India.

Section C

Staying Stopped

Chapter 11

Distract Yourself

**THE HABIT
OF SMOKING**

We have dealt with the most difficult part of quitting – THE ADDICTION TO NICOTINE – but there is more to it than that. To give yourself the greatest possible chance of quitting you must now pay attention to the second important aspect of quitting – THE HABIT OF SMOKING.

★ During the process of smoking a single cigarette, you will take about 10 puffs on that cigarette before you finish it.

★ Hence you put your hand to your mouth about 10 times per cigarette.

★ The average smoker consumes 20 cigarettes per day.

★ So 200 times a day you are putting your hand to your mouth.

★ In one week you are therefore putting your hand to your mouth **1,400** times!

★ Hence in one year you are putting your hand to your mouth more than **73,000** times!

How many years have you smoked for. . .?

Now multiply 73,000 by the number of years that you have smoked for:

73,000 x _____ = _____

That's the number of times you put your hand to your mouth with a cigarette, during your smoking life!

If you smoke more than 20 cigarettes per day, that figure will be even greater. That's an awful lot of 'hand to mouth' activity, which you are going to miss when you stop smoking.

Your mouth will no longer be receiving attention 73,000 times a year.

Your hands will no longer be occupied with this highly repetitive activity. **AND** – your brain will no longer receive its **73,000 shots of nicotine each year.**

When you stop smoking:

(a) Your hands will miss cigarettes.

(b) Your mouth will miss cigarettes.

(c) Your brain will miss cigarettes.

In order to make stopping smoking easier then, you must adopt some plan of action to help yourself. You will have to distract your hands, your mouth and your brain. Before we look at some tried and tested distraction techniques, let me reassure you on the subject of 'cravings'. Smokers planning to give up cigarettes often dread the cravings that might trouble them. They fear a craving coming on, because they imagine that the need to smoke will become stronger and stronger, and eventually become so distressing that the torment will be too much to contend with.

They see themselves becoming tense, edgy and depressed. They dread having to face this stress and if the truth were known they would realise that most of these fears are totally unwarranted. That's right, **totally unwarranted,** because the cravings for a smoke do not last long at all.

A CRAVING DOES NOT LAST MORE THAN 2 TO 3 MINUTES.
THEN THE CRAVING WEARS OFF.

So you see, cravings do not build up and up, and cravings are not on you for hours and hours. They come and go, and because they only last for a few minutes you will, with the help of the following distraction techniques, become proficient at controlling them and clearing them.

DISTRACTION TECHNIQUES

After you have stopped smoking you will experience, at several times of the day, cravings for a smoke. This feeling of needing to have a cigarette can be a very strong desire or a very mild short-lived discomfort.

Whatever the strength of the craving for tobacco the one thing you have to do is distract yourself by keeping busy. YOU must help YOURSELF, and you must appreciate that YOU need to do a lot of the hard work to prevent yourself going back to smoking.

NO-ONE ELSE ON THIS EARTH CAN STOP YOU SMOKING

I want to remind you, at this point, that earlier in the book I stressed that this book cannot stop you smoking. It will help you to stop but it cannot stop you. The decision to stop smoking is yours, and the decision to stay stopped is yours. The final crunch comes when you're dying for a smoke and someone offers you a cigarette. YOU have then to decide whether you're going to have that cigarette or not. The easy solution is to take the cigarette and enjoy it, and tell no-one you've had it. But that is not the right solution; the easy way out is rarely the right way out!

If you are determined to stay off cigarettes then YOU must conquer the cravings by keeping your mind occupied and keeping yourself busy so that thoughts of smoking don't get a chance to trouble you too often.

As mentioned above, your hands, mouth and brain will miss cigarettes and so you must distract your hands, your mouth and your brain.

DISTRACT YOUR HANDS

Your hands have been very involved with your smoking habit – remember that hand to mouth activity 73,000 times a year. On top of all that your hands were involved with the whole ceremony of enjoying the cigarette – searching for the packet, opening it, taking the cigarette out, placing it in your mouth and finally lighting it.

During the process of smoking it, your handling of the cigarette in between puffs, your fiddling with the matches, lighter and cigarette packet, are very important and enjoyable ingredients of the smoking ritual. So when cigarettes go missing from your life your hands will certainly miss them.

REOCCUPY YOUR HANDS

NOTE: You may find some of the ideas to be presented 'silly' and not feasible for you at the present moment. When you stop smoking you will most likely become unreasonable and irrational – you certainly won't remain your normal self, and any of the ideas you will meet from now on could 'save the day' regarding your quitting smoking.

Lots of ideas will be presented to you. I can't tell which ones will suit you as an individual, but do try those suggestions that might help no matter how ridiculous they may seem at the present moment. The ideas that follow have not been concocted by myself: I have learnt these distraction techniques from thousands of smokers over the years. Smokers have taught me that one idea does work and another idea doesn't work, so for your guidance I have included only those suggestions *they* say were useful and worthwhile.

On reading through the distraction techniques your own ideas might occur to you, and if you think of some idea that is useful in helping you to overcome the craving for a smoke, then use it. (Let me know as well, for I learn something new from every smoker that I treat, and any idea that helps one smoker could certainly help others.)

PEN/PENCIL

If possible, carry a pen or pencil with you at all times. A pen or pencil placed between two fingers is a physical replacement for the cigarette; it can be put between the lips as an oral substitute. Some quitters even pretend that it is a cigarette and go through the actions of smoking!

"I'm doing well, I've gone from 30 cigarettes a day down to 5 pencils!" "Great! But don't you find the pencils smell foul when you light them!" "I can cope with the smell, but the splinters are causing havoc with my gums!"

Use the pen or pencil to doodle with, especially when on the phone or when sitting 'passing time'. Write letters to people, write down jobs that you have to do or plan the week ahead.

Office workers might find this idea useful but those in other jobs such as manual work would obviously not follow this idea. Other ideas mentioned later may be more suitable.

DUMMY CIGARETTE

Dummy cigarettes are advertised in several newspapers, two popular brands being 'Apal' and 'Nobac'. These are basically plastic tubes which look like cigarettes but contain menthol crystals. On inhaling, a menthol vapour is released into the mouth. The cigarette must NOT be lit. Some smokers find this a useful item to use when they are giving up cigarettes. It seems to dilute the sudden shock of being totally deprived of the presence of real cigarettes, and many smokers say that out of the corner of their eye it could be a real cigarette, so they don't panic.

However, for other smokers the dummy cigarette would not be suitable as they prefer to remove cigarettes and everything associated with smoking out of their lives. To handle a dummy cigarette would remind them too much of the smoking habit and might even generate cravings. This type of person needs to forget all about cigarettes, so the dummy cigarette would be detrimental rather than helpful.

We are all different and you have to decide what is going to be useful to you as a means of staying off cigarettes. Try the dummy cigarette − if it helps fine, if not discard it.

FIDDLE

As you've been fiddling with cigarettes throughout each day for many years, when you give them up you should try and 'fiddle' with other things to occupy your hands. Smokers in my clinics have advocated the use of many items in this area:

> "Try worry beads, they keep your hands occupied."

> "Rosary beads are useful, they keep my hands busy and I distract my brain at the same time by praying for help to keep off the cigarettes."

> "I've got two pebbles that I roll around my hand every time I feel like a cigarette. The chinking noise drives everybody around me mad, but it seems to calm my nerves."

> "Every time I feel like a cigarette, I fiddle with my wedding ring or earrings. I haven't smoked for eight months."

> "When I stopped smoking I started piano lessons. That soon distracted my hands and my brain."

ROUND-TO-IT

At the back of this book, you will find a list called the 'ROUND-TO-IT' list. On this page you are going to write a list of 'round-to-it' jobs.

Most of us are probably guilty of putting off jobs that ought to be completed. Don't we often say when confronted with some jobs that need doing ... "Oh, I'll get round to it, at the weekend", or "I'll get round to it next week." ... We always seem to be getting 'round to it'!

133

Now you must make a list of those jobs that need doing and write them on the 'ROUND-TO-IT' list. Photocopy the list in this book and put it in a prominent place at home where you and everyone else will see it.

Whenever you feel the strong desire to smoke troubling you, get up and do one of those jobs on the list. You don't have to do the jobs in any set order, just get up and keep yourself busy with any job on the 'ROUND-TO-IT' list. Once you're busy and occupied you are distracted from your problems. So you've decorated the bedrooms twice in the past six weeks! That's fine so long as you haven't smoked!

Putting the 'ROUND-TO-IT' list in a prominent place at home will enable other members of the family to encourage you to keep busy when you start complaining that you're dying for a cigarette. When you've finished all the jobs, they can add more to your list − if you'll let them.

Keeping busy in this manner is vital to prevent yourself returning to the evil weed. This old saying sums it up . . .

"All that is needed for evil to prosper, is that good men do nothing."

DISTRACT YOUR MOUTH

Your lips are very sensitive areas and have been stimulated at least 73,000 times a year by sucking at the end of a cigarette. If you smoke 30 cigarettes a day that total becomes 109,500 times a year, and the 40 per day smoker puts cigarettes into the mouth 146,000 times a year.

Is it very surprising that smokers who quit cigarettes without any guidance or professional help seem to turn to food for comfort? Almost instinctively food becomes the oral substitute for the cigarette. Psychologists call this oral gratification.

CHEWING GUM

Many smokers find chewing gum a useful distraction for the mouth when they quit smoking. Ordinary confectionery chewing gums are effective at keeping the mouth busy, are usually of very low calorie content (vitally important to the new non-smoker), and do seem, through the constant chewing action, to give vent to nervous tension. Notice how many people chew gum avidly when under stress.

Using chewing gum also prevents you putting food in your mouth, and as you may be concerned about possible weight gain on stopping smoking, this factor becomes of prime importance.

Try all the various flavours, to relieve the monotony.

CHOCOLATES, SWEETS ETC

It has been noticed that many smokers go for chocolate when they give up cigarettes. Chocolate contains the stimulant theobromine so some people wonder whether smokers who have given up the drug nicotine, present in tobacco, are seeking another stimulant to replace the nicotine.

Smokers also go for those sweets that have strong tastes, such as mints, liquorice and menthol flavoured items. The strong taste of tobacco has to be replaced by some other strong taste. So to keep your mouth distracted when you give up cigarettes, get in a good stock of strong-tasting sweets.

HOURLY GLUCOSE HELPS SMOKERS QUIT!

Researchers have found that when smokers stop smoking, they experience lower levels of sugar in their blood. This is thought to be due to the absence of nicotine, which can elevate the blood sugar levels. In fact, it is known that diabetics (who have high blood sugar levels) require less insulin when they stop smoking, because their sugar levels drop and they can therefore reduce their insulin requirements.

The symptoms of low blood sugar (known as hypoglycaemia) are nervousness, shakiness, sweating, hunger, confusion, headache and sometimes palpitations. Some smokers who experience these symptoms think that they are due solely to nicotine withdrawal. Well, they're not. These troublesome symptoms can be helped very quickly and simply by having a glucose sweet.

Why not use this knowledge to make quitting easier for yourself? I would recommend that you buy some glucose sweets from your pharmacist or sweet shop, and suck one of these sweets on the hour every hour, during the daytime. You won't need them in the evening, as your blood sugar level should be normal by then. Research has shown that when patients use glucose in this way, they have less severe symptoms on stopping smoking, and therefore have a much higher chance of becoming successful ex-smokers.

Use the 'hourly glucose' idea for the first two weeks of quitting, then you can stop, as it is usually the first fortnight that is the most troublesome time of the quitting process.

The thought of stuffing oneself with high calorie foods such as sweets causes a lot of ex-smokers some concern, especially the women ex-smokers.

I would advise you to eat whatever you fancy during your FIRST TWO WEEKS of quitting cigarettes, be it sweets, chocolates, biscuits, cream cakes or whatever. I don't believe many smokers can give up cigarettes and diet at the same time. They often fail at both, when dividing their attention between the two problems.

When giving up cigarettes, I have found that the most sensible and therefore successful technique is to concentrate all your energies on one problem at a time.

At first, your most important and difficult problem is getting the cigarettes out of your life.

When you have jumped that first hurdle − and only then − you may jump the next hurdle and put all your determination into losing any weight that you may have gained by stopping smoking.

If you have been successful at giving up smoking, you will feel very confident with yourself, and controlling your weight will seem an easier task to cope with. Remember that I have, in this book, provided you with a very effective diet to follow, called the 'FAT FAREWELL' WEIGHT LOSS PLAN, which you will be using from the fourth week after your Quit Day.

So during those first two weeks of no cigarettes eat whatever you want, but only for two weeks, then you can be more selective in what you eat. It is important to allow yourself treats such as cream cakes, biscuits and chocolates. These are rewards to yourself for not giving in to cigarettes, and psychologically it is vital that you reward yourself, maybe at the end of each meal or the end of the day, with something sweet and tasty.

By doing this for only the first two weeks of quitting you won't put on too much weight. So for now, please DO NOT DIET AND QUIT SMOKING AT THE SAME TIME. Do one or the other but don't do both together.

FRUIT JUICES

Instead of starting each morning with a cough and a cigarette, why don't you start your Quit Day with a glass of fresh orange juice by your bedside? Throughout the day try and drink more fresh fruit juice instead of resorting to smelly unhealthy cigarettes.

Fresh fruit juice contains Vitamin C, which smokers especially need, because this vitamin acts as a detoxifying agent, breaking down the various impurities present in the body. As a smoker you will have plenty of those in your body and the sooner you're rid of them the better. So to help your body recover from its long-term exposure to tobacco smoke, drink more fruit juice and eat more fresh fruit and vegetables as well.

Celery sticks and carrots are popular with some smokers who are quitting, but they do make such a noise in the library or the cinema!

Other items that smokers have sworn by as good things to try to distract the mouth have been such things as peanuts, cinnamon sticks and liquorice root. The list could be endless, but you think of what could help you and use it as long as it is harmless.

CAFFEINE AND SMOKING

Did you know that nicotine helps your internal chemistry to break down caffeine in the body? This is an extremely important point to keep in mind, because most smokers like their tea and coffee, and when they give up smoking they continue to drink tea and coffee, sometimes in greater amounts than when they smoked. When you stop smoking your previously high blood nicotine level falls so that caffeine from tea and coffee is no longer broken down as rapidly. Your blood levels of caffeine then jump up.

It has been found that the caffeine levels in a person who has just stopped smoking can be 4 times higher than their previous levels. Such high doses of caffeine can make a person feel edgy, anxious and shaky – symptoms that might be attributed to tobacco withdrawal, or to the nicotine patch or gum, when in fact they are not.

So here is another useful hint to make stopping smoking as easy as possible:

★ On stopping smoking, change over to decaffeinated coffee and tea (yes, you can get decaffeinated tea in several supermarkets!)

★ If you don't like decaffeinated drinks, you will have to drink your tea and coffee weaker, or have less cups per day.

Don't forget that other drinks such as Coke and even hot chocolate may contain caffeine. You can even get decaffeinated Coke!

DISTRACT YOUR BRAIN

Your brain is where the cravings really come from, and all the troublesome effects of stopping smoking are produced by the brain missing both the drug nicotine and the deeply ingrained habit of a lifetime. Distracting your brain can be done without too much difficulty, as long as YOU make the conscious decision to do something YOURSELF.

ROUND-TO-IT

The 'ROUND-TO-IT' list has already been mentioned as a distraction for the hands. It is also an ideal distraction for the brain.

Imagine you have had a bad day at work, you have also stopped smoking and you've just come home and had your evening meal. After your meal, maybe you like to sit down in an easy chair with a cup of tea or coffee, and watch the TV. So you do this, but something is missing – there is no cigarette. And wouldn't it be nice just to have one now, especially after such a rotten day at work! You can feel the craving coming on, can't you? What would you give for a cigarette now? What wouldn't you give?

The brain is craving for tobacco, so instead of sitting there dying for a smoke and feeling sorry for yourself, you must get up and DO SOMETHING. Take the dog for a walk ... or ... use your 'ROUND-TO-IT' list and do one of those jobs AT ONCE.

If you don't, you know what will happen, especially if other people are smoking in the same room!

It might help if one of the jobs on your 'ROUND-TO-IT' list is:

"Change position of chairs in lounge."

This is recommended because you probably sit in the same chair in the same place in the lounge every evening. Your routine then will consist of reaching out automatically to the coffee table for your pack of cigarettes, without even looking. This pure reflex action will reveal that the cigarettes are not there and you will wonder where the heck are they. You have actually forgotten for an instant that you no longer smoke – and then when the truth dawns upon you the craving starts. Changing the position of the furniture can help eliminate this troublesome problem.

Office workers can also gain from this idea, if it is a reasonable thing to do without affecting too many other people.

PASTIMES/ HOBBIES

If you enjoy reading then you appreciate that you can 'lose' yourself in a good book. A good novel can make you oblivious to your surroundings, and time just flies if you are immersed in a good story. So spend some of that money you have saved on two or three bestsellers and curl up.

People with hobbies are fortunate because they too can immerse themselves in their favourite pastime. They switch off completely whilst enjoying their hobby, whatever it is. If you don't have a hobby then you should seriously think about starting one now that you have stopped smoking. A hobby is a great distraction and is extremely therapeutic. Maybe now's the time to start something that you've really fancied doing for a long time. You think about it.

RELAXATION

Whenever you smoked a cigarette it made you feel relaxed and at ease. Tobacco contains nicotine which does have some relaxing effects but you also become relaxed when smoking because when you smoked your cigarette you actually did some **slow deep breathing.**

Just watch a smoker with a cigarette. Notice how they slowly inhale the smoke, then hold it for a second or two and slowly breathe it out. The whole process is one of controlled slow deep breathing. Anyone undergoing slow deep breathing is going to end up feeling relaxed, so why not do that without cigarette smoke going down into your lungs? In other words . . . **'smoke fresh air'.**

Whenever you feel like a cigarette, tell yourself to go ahead and have a smoke but only smoke 'fresh air'. Pretend you have a cigarette in your mouth and inhale very slowly, counting to yourself . . . ONE, . . . TWO, . . . THREE, then hold your breath for a few seconds, then breathe out slowly . . . ONE, . . . TWO, . . . THREE.

As you breathe out slowly notice how relaxed you are feeling. It's as if you are flushing out the tension and craving from your body with each breath out.

Every time you breathe out you are going to feel even more relaxed than before. After half a dozen slow deep breaths you should feel more relaxed and the craving should not bother you. So let's try it together . . .

SLOW DEEP BREATHING

Try some slow deep breathing with me now.

Take in a SLOW deep breath now, filling all your lungs with air and counting ... ONE ... TWO ... THREE. As you breathe in feel the tension building up in the muscles of your neck and shoulders.

Now HOLD your breath and feel the tension building up across your chest.

After a couple of seconds then release your breath and SLOWLY breathe out again, counting ... ONE ... TWO ... THREE, feeling the tension draining from you as you count.

Most of my successful ex-smoking patients tell me that this 'Deep Breathing' helps a lot. Try it again and again, anywhere you like, for no-one need know that you're doing it! The more you practise this breathing routine the more effective it will become at relaxing you and removing the cravings.

OR PUT IT ANOTHER WAY –
"SMOKE FRESH AIR"!

EXERCISE

As you are now going to be a healthier person as a result of stopping smoking, let's try and improve your health even further and more quickly. Why not try some gentle exercise every day, such as going for a walk or a gentle 'jog', or swimming? If you have a heart or lung condition, or a circulation problem then you should check with your doctor before embarking on any exercise programme.

After a few weeks of not smoking you might get a pleasant surprise at your lack of tiredness.

You will see in the chapter on the 'FAT FAREWELL' WEIGHT LOSS PLAN, that exercise is discussed further, and it is an integral part of the slimming plan.

Exercise makes you feel better ... but do it with care.

IN SUMMARY

Many distraction techniques for hand, mouth and brain have been introduced to you. Some may not suit you, but do try and think of other techniques that might suit you. Anything that helps you to stay off cigarettes is worth trying.

QUITTERS' STORIES

Miss K.N., shop assistant...

"Every time I felt like a cigarette, I went off to the ladies room and gargled with a mouthwash. I think I've tried every make of mouthwash available on the market. It was nice to have a clean fresh mouth and a clean pink tongue. The manager wasn't too happy with me during the first week of quitting, as I was forever leaving the counter."

Mr. L.B., crane operator...

"One disadvantage of stopping smoking for me was the loss of sleep. After giving up cigarettes I suffered from insomnia for about two weeks... and ironically, the disadvantage became an attractive advantage... my sex life improved! Well you couldn't just lie there thinking of cigarettes, you had to distract yourself. My breath was no longer stale, and I had more energy... Wow, was I glad I stopped smoking."

Mr. W.D., retired...

"I helped myself to get over the desire to smoke by making a very long list of 'ROUND-TO-IT' jobs. As I am retired I had plenty of time on my hands, and for that very reason I dreaded giving up smoking and being stuck at home all day. However the list of jobs has kept me very busy and out of mischief,... I'm like a human whirlwind... non-stop activity."

Miss A.R., student and non-smoker... (A stunning, 'suggestive' blonde.)

"If smokers can't think of anything better to do with their hands and mouth than smoke cigarettes, then I feel very sorry for them!"

IF SMOKERS CAN'T THINK OF ANYTHING BETTER TO DO WITH THEIR HANDS AND MOUTH THAN SMOKE CIGARETTES, THEN I FEEL VERY SORRY FOR THEM!!

Chapter 12

The 'Fat Farewell' Weight Loss Plan

WORRIED ABOUT PUTTING ON WEIGHT?

One of the most difficult problems for many people who have recently stopped smoking is weight gain. The reasons for putting on weight are simple and shouldn't bring about an overreaction. You gain weight for four reasons:

(1) Instead of putting cigarettes into your mouth, you put food in as a direct substitute. Remember that hand to mouth activity of 73,000 times a year for a 20 per day smoker?

(2) When you give up smoking, your sense of smell and sense of taste improve. Food tastes and smells better, so you eat more.

(3) On stopping smoking you miss nicotine, which has an appetite suppressant effect. Therefore, when you give up the cigarettes your appetite improves.

(4) Nicotine is also said to have a metabolic effect, that is it helps to 'burn up' calories. When you stop smoking you no longer take nicotine into your body, so you do not 'burn up' calories. These unburnt calories are then stored as fat.

HOW THE USE OF NICOTINE GUM AND PATCHES HELP AVOID WEIGHT GAIN

These last two points relating to nicotine are not too relevant to the smoker who gives up cigarettes using the Nicotine Reduction Therapies.

If the gum is used then the ex-smoker receives a small amount of nicotine with its associated effects on appetite and the body's internal chemistry every time the gum is chewed. Anybody who uses nicotine gum regularly throughout the day tends not to eat too much extra food on stopping smoking because their mouth is busy chewing for most of the day. Try eating in between meals with a mouth full of chewing gum!

Those using the nicotine skin patches, especially the 24-hour patches, should find that they don't put on too much weight. This is thought to be a benefit of having nicotine going into the body continually over the day and night, thus providing its appetite suppressant effects on a continuous basis. And you may remember, in one particular study those patients who used the nicotine skin patch only put on a few ounces in three months, while those who were given a placebo (a blank patch containing no nicotine) gained over 9lbs!

VANITY COUNTS

The weight gain experienced after stopping smoking is usually rapid. It occurs within 4-6 weeks of giving up cigarettes and is very disheartening for the ex-smoker. This rapid weight gain is often cited as the cause of many women ex-smokers going back to their cigarettes. It is a fact of life that, for many, vanity is more important than health!

A TIP ON HOW TO WEIGH YOURSELF AFTER GIVING UP CIGARETTES:

Weigh yourself

- only once a week, every week

- at the same time of day

- on the same day each week, using the same scales

- in the same room

- at the same spot

- in the same clothes (preferably unclothed).

Record your weight every week, whilst you follow this weight loss plan, on the 'FAT FAREWELL' WEIGHT LOSS CHART at the end of this chapter.

DO NOT ATTEMPT TO DIET AND STOP SMOKING AT THE SAME TIME

During your early weeks of quitting smoking, concentrate purely on living without your cigarettes. After the first month, you could then direct your energies towards shifting the excess weight that you may have gained. Most ex-smokers have found the following diet extremely useful.

So 4 weeks after giving up your cigarettes, if you have gained weight and want to lose it, put yourself onto the 'FAT FAREWELL' WEIGHT LOSS PLAN. I wrote this plan for the TV programme *This Morning*, and it proved very popular indeed with over 100,000 viewers sending in for it!

This plan evolved over many years as there was an obvious and desperate need to give help to those smokers attending my 'Stop Smoking' Clinics, who had successfully quit smoking but were becoming very disheartened by their rapidly increasing weight gain. A simple and very effective routine was needed – I hope you find it useful.

The FAT FAREWELL PLAN provides guidance in three important areas:

1. What to eat.

2. How to eat.

3. Exercise.

THE 'FAT FAREWELL' WEIGHT LOSS PLAN

1.

WHAT TO EAT

★ Where amounts are not stipulated, any amount of that item is allowed – yes, that's right – **any amount!**

★ Where fish is mentioned, any fish can be eaten except for tinned fish in oil. Tinned fish in brine is allowed.

★ Where meat is mentioned, any meat without the fat is acceptable. Sausage meats are **not** allowed.

BREAKFAST:

1. Fresh fruit or glass of fruit juice.

2. One egg with one slice of brown toast.

   or

   One average helping of unsweetened cereal.

3. Tea or coffee – any amount.

LUNCH:

1. Low calorie soup − one serving.

2. Lean meat − any amount.

3. Mixed salad − any amount. Note that meat and salad can be taken as a sandwich with two slices of wholemeal bread.

4. Single fresh fruit − 1 apple or 1 orange etc.

5. Tea or coffee − any amount.

EVENING MEAL:

1. Meat of your choice − any amount.

or

Fish of your choice − any amount.

2. Two fresh vegetables − any amount.

3. One baked potato or small helping of boiled potatoes.

or

Small helping of boiled rice.

or

Small helping of pasta.

4. Fresh fruit or very low fat fruit yoghurt.

5. Tea or coffee − any amount.

INSTEAD OF: TAKE:

Sugar .... Low calorie sweeteners.

Milk .... Semi-skimmed milk – 1 pint/day.

White bread .. Wholemeal bread – 3 slices/day.

Cheese .... Cottage cheese.

Butter .... Low-fat spreads – used
                             sparingly.

Soft drinks .... Low calorie drinks.

Fried food ..... Grilled, poached, baked, boiled
                             or steamed.

Bananas .... Any other fresh fruit.

SNACKS

Ideally – there should be no eating between meals!

★ If tempted nibble on raw carrots, celery, radishes, pickled onions or melon.

★ Drinking plenty of low calorie soft drinks throughout the day can help a great deal. Bovril, Oxo, Marmite or mineral waters are also recommended. If you can't include food, then drink plenty of low calorie fluids. Tea and coffee may have to be decaffeinated if you want to avoid high caffeine blood levels (see earlier). With tea and coffee use low calorie sweeteners and no more than the daily allowance of milk.

FORBIDDEN FOODS

★ Avoid sweets, sugar, chocolate, jam, cakes, pastry, biscuits.

★ Avoid fat: eg. fat on meat, skin on poultry, butter, cream.

★ Avoid all fried food.

★ Avoid thick soups, thick sauces, mayonnaise.

★ If alcohol must be taken, restrict intake and drink dry wines instead of sweet drinks and shorts. Low alcohol beers and other low calorie alcohol drinks should be considered.

(Note: 2 glasses of wine = 1 pint of beer or 1 single whisky.)

153

2.

HOW TO EAT

1. Before eating any food ask yourself this question:

   "AM I REALLY HUNGRY?"

   Halfway to two thirds way through your meal, ask yourself the same question. If the answer is yes, continue eating.

   If the answer is no ... STOP EATING ... put the food aside ... leave the table and do something to keep yourself busy. This is not easy to do but if you understand why you are doing it, you can succeed.

   What you are doing is DISTRACTING YOURSELF FROM THE EATING PROCESS.

2. Food should be eaten off small plates, to give the impression of full or over-flowing plates.

3. Whilst eating allow yourself fully to enjoy the sight and the smell of the food.

4. Eat your food SLOWLY, appreciating the full taste of every mouthful – savour the flavour!

ACCEPTABLE WEIGHT RANGES FOR MALE AND FEMALE

MALE

Height in Shoes		Weight Lower Level		Upper Level	
ft	in	st	lb	st	lb
5	2	9	0 –	10	1
5	3	9	3 –	10	4
5	4	9	6 –	10	8
5	5	9	9 –	10	12
5	6	9	12 –	11	2
5	7	10	2 –	11	7
5	8	10	7 –	11	12
5	9	10	11 –	12	2
5	10	11	1 –	12	6
5	11	11	5 –	12	11
6	0	11	10 –	13	2
6	1	12	0 –	13	7
6	2	12	5 –	13	12
6	3	12	10 –	14	3
6	4	13	0 –	14	8

FEMALE

Height in Shoes		Weight Lower Level		Upper Level	
ft	in	st	lb	st	lb
4	10	7	6 –	8	7
4	11	7	8 –	8	10
5	0	7	11 –	8	13
5	1	8	0 –	9	2
5	2	8	3 –	9	5
5	3	8	6 –	9	8
5	4	8	9 –	9	12
5	5	8	13 –	10	2
5	6	9	3 –	10	6
5	7	9	7 –	10	10
5	8	9	11 –	11	0
5	9	10	1 –	11	4
5	10	10	5 –	11	9
5	11	10	9 –	12	0
6	0	10	13 –	12	5

BELOW LOWER LEVEL – UNDERWEIGHT
OVER UPPER LEVEL – OVERWEIGHT

'THE FAT FAREWELL WEIGHT LOSS CHART'

NAME: _____ Year: 19											
Jan	Feb	Mar	Apr	May	Jun	Jul	Aug	Sep	Oct	Nov	Dec
1											
2											
3											
4											
5											
6											
7											
8											
9											
10											
11											
12											
13											
14											
15											
16											
17											
18											
19											
20											
21											
22											
23											
24											
25											
26											
27											
28											
29											
30											
31											

Weigh yourself:
- only once a week
- every week
- at the same time of day
- on the same day each week
- on the same scales
- in the same room
- at the same spot
- in the same clothes (preferably unclothed).

3.

EXERCISE   To lose weight you must decrease your calorie intake and increase your calorie output − that is eat less food *and* do more exercise, more aptly described as:

DIET AND DO IT   There are many people who eat 5,000 to 6,000 calories every day yet they remain thin healthy people − who are these lucky people? − Athletes!

Athletes exercise regularly every day and yet have a vast intake of calories. Two years ago I interviewed Steve Cram and I was surprised at his intake of 6,000 calories a day. He is slim because he runs every single day. We really can learn from this.

So if you need to lose weight, you must take more exercise, on a regular basis. By exercise, I don't mean strenuous running or jogging, I mean just walking. If you just went walking around your neighbourhood on a regular basis, no matter what the weather is like, you would lose weight. I have seen several patients who have suffered a heart attack, and were then advised by their specialist to lose some weight − and they all did, because they did what he advised them to do: "Go out and buy a puppy!" The dog had to be taken out for a walk every single day and the lucky dog owner lost weight.

Keep walking in mind as a form of weight-losing exercise. Look at people who do walk a lot in the course of their jobs − postmen! How often do you see a fat postman, or a fat milkman for that matter? So get walking regularly!

THREE TIPS THAT MIGHT HELP YOU

★ Exercising before a meal can actually make you feel less hungry!

★ Exercising will make you feel physically fitter and mentally more alert and more determined in your whole approach to life.

★ Increasing your exercise activities can raise your metabolic rate (the speed of the body's internal chemistry) so that you burn off calories **even when you're not exercising.**

To achieve effective weight loss whilst following this plan you **MUST** –

EXERCISE AT LEAST 3 TIMES PER WEEK.

EXERCISE FOR AT LEAST 20 MINUTES AT EACH SESSION.

Twenty minutes is a long time to do non-stop exercise, so don't be too enthusiastic at first. Start **gentle** walking non-stop – 10 minutes out and 10 minutes back – without any rests.

Then gently increase your pace until you can do brisk non-stop walking for 20 minutes. You may even feel brave enough to try a **gentle** jog, for 20 minutes. If you feel any pains or discomfort, stop and rest.

Any exercise can be pursued, as long as it follows the rules of this slimming plan, in other words:

– at least 20 minutes and

– at least 3 times a week.

If you can increase your exercise time beyond 20 minutes, do so.

If you can increase your exercise sessions to more than 3 times per week, do so. **The exercise routines suggested here must be additional to the exercise you are taking at present.**

IN SUMMARY   This slimming plan has advised you on three aspects of weight loss:

1. What to eat.

2. How to eat.

3. Exercise.

To lose weight you *must* devote all your attention and energies to **all three** aspects, especially the exercise component. Even gentle regular walking will do the trick. So do it!

QUITTERS' STORIES

Ms. E.R., nursery attendant . . .

"I decided to ignore any weight gain for the first month. It was great because I allowed myself to eat everything that I wanted as a reward for not smoking. I binged on chocolates and cream cakes ... it was bliss! Actually after the first 2 weeks I stopped overdoing it as I didn't need to eat as much. But it was useful to be able to replace the cigarettes with something else that gave me pleasure ... luscious high calorie food!

"During the first week I think I went through a 'panic eating phase'. When cigarettes were not there, I panicked and therefore ate and ate. I told friends I was on a 'sea-food' diet — I see food and I eat it!

"So my routine was . . . 2 weeks eating everything . . . followed by 2 weeks eating normally . . . followed by 2 weeks dieting.

"In the 2 weeks of dieting I lost all the weight I had gained during those first 4 weeks of quitting smoking (10lbs)."

Mrs. D.R., caterer . . .

"I had read somewhere that you would have had to be nearly twice your normal body weight to face the same risk to your health as you face by smoking. I therefore stopped the cigarettes first and enjoyed my food as a replacement. Then I felt very confident and so I tackled the weight problem next. I solved both problems, now I feel great!"

TOBACCO TRIVIA

Here is a selection of 'Tobacco Trivia' questions to test your knowledge, and hopefully, to keep you in a light-hearted mood, whilst you while away your smoke-free hours!

QUESTIONS:

1. A few years ago 'Perrier' water was temporarily taken off the market because one batch was found to be contaminated with benzene – a cancer-causing agent. The concentration of benzene in the water was 4.7 micrograms per litre. What is the concentration in a cigarette?

a. 10 mcgm b. 55 mcgm c. 190 mcgm

2. What percentage of British people smoke?

3. How many chemicals are there in cigarette smoke?

4. What is one effect of smoking on male sexual function?

5. The tobacco industry spends £100 million a year on advertising cigarettes. To counteract this the Government spends how much on anti-smoking campaigns?

a. £4 million   b. £85 million
c. £200 million

6. Who was the English monarch who tried to stamp out smoking, by increasing the import on tobacco by 4000%?

7. How many miscarriages occur each year as a result of maternal smoking?

a. 400   b. 1,200   c. 7,500

8. 'Sidestream' smoke contains more tar, nicotine and carbon monoxide than 'mainstream' smoke. True or false?

9. Smoking kills more people per year than alcohol, heroin, cocaine, murders, road accidents, suicides, fires and AIDS combined.
True or false?

10. Is the incidence of lung cancer increasing in women?

11. What did Yul Brynner, Humphrey Bogart, Pat Phoenix, Betty Grable, Buster Keaton, Jack Benny, Nat 'King' Cole, John Wayne and Walt Disney all have in common?

12. How many people under the legal age of 16 start smoking in the UK each year?

a. 204,000   b. 77,000   c. 137,000

ANSWERS:
1. 190 mcgm in one cigarette! The average smoker of 20 cigarettes a day is taking in 3,800 mcgm of benzene! 2. About 30%. 3. 4000. 4. Impotence. 5. £4 million. 6. King James I (1566 – 1625). 7. 7,500. 8. True. 9. True. Deaths from smoking total 110,000 per year. 10. Yes. In some countries it now kills more women than breast cancer. 11. They all died of lung cancer. 12. 137,000. Which is just enough to replace the number of people who die each year from the same habit!

Chapter 13

No Thanks...
I Don't Smoke!

I AM NOW
A NON-
SMOKER

From your Quit Day onwards always class yourself as a non-smoker rather than an ex-smoker. You will feel better calling yourself a NON-smoker rather than an EX-smoker!

During your early weeks of giving up cigarettes you will be very vulnerable and easy prey for anyone who wants you to go back to smoking – and some smokers will want to do just that to you. About 70 per cent of smokers admit that they would like to stop if they could, and about three quarters of all smokers have tried at least twice to give up their cigarettes and failed.

The message to be gained then, from these figures is:

MOST SMOKERS HAVE TRIED TO STOP AND FAILED.

Therefore, **BEWARE SMOKERS!**

Many of your smoking friends and smoking family members may have tried to stop at some time in the past, and not been successful. Now that you are winning, there may be some feelings of petty jealousy developing. After all, you are succeeding where they have not, and smokers don't like that.

When you stop smoking you soon find out who your friends are. You may be quite surprised to discover that the very persons you expected to be supportive are the ones who are offering you cigarettes after you've given up. Non-smokers and ex-smokers won't offer you cigarettes. Only smokers will offer cigarettes to you. So are you to avoid smokers completely? Well you can't do this in practice so you have to learn how to cope with smokers.

HERE ARE A FEW USEFUL LITTLE TIPS

At first DON'T TELL EVERYONE you know that you are going to stop or have stopped smoking.

During your first 2 to 3 weeks of giving up cigarettes, play it very low key. Try and keep the fact that you are stopping to yourself. Obviously close friends and family will know, but you should certainly not let others know you are quitting until you've got at least the first couple of weeks behind you. Some authorities recommend that you tell all and sundry about your giving up smoking, in the belief that it will help you stay off cigarettes. The loss of face and the shame created by your returning to smoking will, they claim, prevent you from smoking again . . . who are they kidding?

When you are troubled by the strong urge to smoke, that desire can be so overpowering that loss of pride is the last thing on your mind. You have to appreciate that not only are you trying to give up a deep-seated and long-standing habit but also an addiction to the drug nicotine which is present in cigarette smoke. This addiction can be very strong indeed. Let me give you a very interesting example.

One particular group of patients who had developed lung cancer as a result of smoking underwent surgery to remove the cancerous lung. These patients were told that their cancer was caused by smoking and they all gave up their cigarettes. When followed up 12 months later nearly half of them (47 per cent) had started smoking again. They only had one lung left, and they had been fortunate enough to have escaped an unpleasant death from cancer – yet they had started smoking again!

Such is the strength of the addiction to tobacco, and the powerful hold that it has over its users.

That hold can create such a strong need for a smoke that you just don't care what people think of you. YOU are the one who is suffering and YOU want a cigarette. So you have one (just the one, you tell yourself), and unfortunately you could be back on your way to smoking again.

So during your first couple of weeks of quitting just quietly get on with the business of not smoking, and then after that fortnight or so, gradually let it be known that you have stopped smoking. By that time you will probably be over the worst, you will feel more confident and you will find it easier to cope with smokers offering you cigarettes.

If possible, whenever people offer you a cigarette, reply by saying:

"NO THANKS . . . I DON'T SMOKE."

You'll really feel proud of yourself and it will give a great boost to your confidence. So, if saying "No thanks, *I* don't smoke!" makes you feel superior ... great! Do it!

If you are offered cigarettes by people who know you do smoke, then tell a little white lie by saying:

"No thanks, I've just had one," or "No thanks ... later maybe."

Imagine that you are at a social function or party, and you're in a small group amongst whom are a few smokers. The alcohol is flowing freely, and of course, before you quit smoking, cigarettes and alcohol went together, didn't they? Whenever you had a drink you tended to have a smoke. Now with just a drink in your hand and no cigarette, it feels odd. It just doesn't feel right and you are decidedly uncomfortable.

Nevertheless you're coping, but someone in your little group offers you a cigarette and your reply is − "No thank you, I've just given them up." At that point you can guarantee that one smoker in the group will ask you about your smoking habit and giving up. The questions you will probably face will include:

"When did you stop smoking?"

"How many were you smoking before you gave it up?"

"How long have you smoked for?"

"Goodness, aren't you dying for a cigarette?"

Of course you're dying for a cigarette. They're enjoying their cigarettes, and blowing the smoke your way as they ask these questions. As each question is asked, your desire to smoke seems to become stronger and stronger – in other words, you have become the centre of attention and your quitting smoking has become the topic of conversation. If this conversation continues you'll end up killing someone in order to get a cigarette!

The longer the conversation dwells upon smoking, cigarettes and you quitting, the worse you're going to feel. The solution to the problem of smokers offering you cigarettes, then, lies in your reply.

Whenever possible respond by saying "NO THANKS, I DON'T SMOKE." and then *you* change the subject and talk about some programme on TV last night or some other topic that might get others talking. On no account let the conversation centre on smoking or you giving up your cigarettes.

This advice should be followed mainly during the early weeks of quitting. After those first 2 to 3 weeks you should be able to cope with smokers and all the temptation that they will put your way.

If you feel tempted to have a cigarette at any time, just remember the suffering that you have gone through to become a non-smoker. Only you know what hardship you have suffered in living without your cigarettes. Don't let all that go to waste just for one cigarette.

Although you may feel desperate for a cigarette, the satisfaction you get by giving in to the craving and lighting up can be very disappointing. Many a smoker has admitted that they could have kicked themselves for giving in to the craving, for it just wasn't worth it.

The desire for a smoke is often out of all proportion to the satisfaction you feel after lighting up. So don't give in, it's not worth it. REMEMBER:

"No thanks, I don't smoke." ... "Did you see that programme on TV last night ...?" etc

"No thanks, I'll have one later." ... "Are you going away on holiday this year ...?" etc

"No thanks, I've just had one."

QUITTERS' STORIES

Mr. J.F., musician . . .

"It felt very strange at first, saying 'No thanks, I don't smoke.' But I soon got a kick out of saying that to people, and it really did make me feel quite superior. I must have become quite a bore to my friends, for whilst in their company (and some were smokers) I would repeat over and over, in different tones of voice and accents, 'No thanks, I don't smoke. . . . 'No thanks, I don't smoke.' Now I do understand that ex-smokers can be a real pain!''

Mr. P.D., office worker . . .

"The office I work in is a modern open plan unit. The practice in the office is for the smokers to take turns in handing out their cigarettes. As each smoker took a cigarette out for himself he would throw one across the desks to each of the other smokers.

"When I decided to stop, all of the smokers in the office stopped throwing a cigarette my way, except for one . . . don't you always get one that insists on making you have a cigarette when you've just given up?

"This one awkward smoker would not accept my refusal to have a cigarette, as every time it came to his turn he would still throw me a cigarette despite my pleas of 'No thanks, I don't smoke.' I decided to take the next cigarette from him, and he waited with bated breath expecting me to light it. I broke it in half, crushed it up in my hand and threw it into the bin. He never tempted me again with another cigarette! You can lose some friends that way, but there again who needs friends like that when you are trying like heck to quit smoking?''

TOBACCO TRIVIA

Here is a selection of 'Tobacco Trivia' questions to test your knowledge, and, hopefully, to keep you in a light-hearted mood as you while away your smoke-free hours!

QUESTIONS:

1. What percentage of the inhaled particles of cigarette smoke remain in the lungs?

2. How can smoking cause gangrene of the leg, leading to amputation?

3. The children of mothers who smoke are more prone to develop what conditions?

4. When was the link between smoking and lung cancer discovered?

5. How many smokers feel they would like to quit the habit?
a. 30%   b. 40%
c. 50%   d. 80%

6. If cigarette tar is painted on the skins of mice, what happens?

7. How many cigarettes per day are produced by a modern cigarette manufacturing machine?

8. What other types of cancer, besides lung cancer, are associated with smoking?

9. Who, when dying from lung cancer, gave a message to young people in a pre-recorded film, saying "Now that I'm gone, I tell you . . . whatever you do, just don't smoke"?

10. What percentage of people having leg amputations for bad circulation are smokers?

11. What effect does smoking have on the sensations of taste and smell?

12. Young children of smoking parents inhale the nicotine equivalent to smoking how many cigarettes a year?
a. 5   b. 20   c. 40   d. 80

13. Research has shown that most people who stay off cigarettes for 3 – 4 months stay off cigarettes for good. True or false?

ANSWERS:

1. 85%. 2. By narrowing and blocking the blood vessels to the leg. 3. The children of smoking parents are more prone to cot death, meningitis, physical deformities, eg. cleft palate, hare lip, asthma, abnormalities of the nervous system, deafness (from glue ear), pneumonia, chest infections, allergies and childhood cancers such as leukaemia and Hodgkin's disease. 4. Early 1950's. 5. 80%. 6. Research consistently shows that the vast majority of smokers are unhappy about their habit and want to quit. 6. They develop skin cancer. 7. 6 million. 8. Cancer of the lip, tongue, mouth, larynx (voice box), oesophagus (gullet), kidney, bladder and pancreas. 9. Yul Brynner. 10. 90%. 11. It reduces both. 12. 80 cigarettes. Studies have shown that 'passive' or 'side-stream' smoking can have a serious effect on non-smokers. A study in England showed that a child could effectively inhale nicotine equivalent to 80 cigarettes per year. If you and both parents smoked, have weighed up the risks of smoking and are happy to continue what choice do your children have? 13. True.

Chapter 14

If You Don't Succeed . . .

THE FUTURE

I don't wish to sound pessimistic but there is a great deal of truth in the saying − "Once a smoker always a smoker!"

Once you have stopped smoking don't be tempted to try a cigar on a special occasion. Many ex-smokers have had just a 'social' cigar that became 3 . . . then 5 cigars a day, which eventually led them to smoking cigarettes again.

YOU CANNOT HAVE 'JUST THE ONE' CIGARETTE (OR CIGAR).
IT'S TOO DANGEROUS TO CHANCE IT.

If you don't smoke . . . you do NOT smoke, even a single cigarette! Don't be too bothered by the ex-smoker who tells you that it is 10 years since he gave them up and only the other day he was dying for a cigarette. To you that sounds as if the cravings for a smoke are still as strong 10 years after quitting. I can reassure you that this is not the case.

What he probably meant was that he just caught the whiff of a cigarette as someone passed him and that he felt, just at that moment in time, it would have been nice to try the taste of a cigarette again − but he didn't. In other words it was not a troublesome craving hanging around him for hours but a very transient and passing memory that didn't cause him any bother whatsoever.

So don't be tempted − always think of what you have gone through in your struggle to get this far. You have achieved the state of becoming a non-smoker through hard work and sheer determination.

So don't BLOW it . . . for a SUCK on a cig!

LET'S BE REALISTIC

For many people the process of giving up cigarettes involves quitting, then possibly slipping back and having the odd one or two, then keeping on going and maybe having another odd cigarette here and there, until they eventually become long-term ex-smokers.

Most long-term ex-smokers are smokers who have failed to stop smoking at several previous attempts. They tell me that they kept on trying to give up smoking, and then for some reason or other things just seemed to go right in that last attempt at quitting.

There's never an ideal time to quit smoking. Can't you just guarantee that at the very moment when you have planned to give up cigarettes, things will start going wrong in your life? Typical, isn't it!

Well maybe during this attempt at quitting you have not found it too easy to cope without your cigarettes. Perhaps you are under a great deal of stress at work or at home. If you have financial worries, domestic problems or any other type of stress in your life at the present moment, then it is NOT the ideal time for you to try and stop smoking.

If it has been a nightmare for you to stop smoking at this attempt and you have not been successful at quitting do not get despondent or downhearted. Maybe now is not the perfect time for you to give up.

If you have not been able to stop, then learn by your mistakes. Did you take cigarettes offered to you at that party or did you find a cigarette in the bedside drawer? Did you ignore the instructions given to you in this book, say about quitting with your partner or with a friend, and were they the cause of you going back to smoking?

Whatever went wrong, you know what it was and you can learn from those mistakes. Next time you try to give up smoking you won't make the same mistakes again.

If you do fail at one attempt to stop smoking, that's not the end of the world. You can have another go at another time. Come back to this book at a later date, maybe when there is less stress in your life, and when you feel more confident about quitting. You can try as many times as you like – WHO'S COUNTING?

**IF AT FIRST YOU DON'T SUCCEED –
QUIT . . . QUIT . . . AGAIN!**

"IF AT FIRST YOU DON'T SUCCEED, QUIT, QUIT AGAIN"

QUITTERS' STORIES

Mr. J.J., computer operator ...

"To avoid becoming negative, I emphasized to myself all the benefits I was feeling after stopping smoking. I made a list of all the improvements I was experiencing, it was rather like the old self-improvement courses ... 'each and every day I'm feeling better and better.' Despite all the positive reinforcement I made a silly mistake and relapsed into smoking again. I decided to learn by my mistake (which was to try 'just the one' cigarette) and I tried again, resolving not to smoke ANY cigarettes after Q-Day. If you don't succeed DO try again, for it can be easier next time round."

Mrs. N.C., telephonist ...

"I attempted to give up my cigarettes at a bad time. I was going through divorce proceedings at the time, and it was hell. I decided to try again when my life circumstances improved. One year later I gave up smoking whilst away on holiday in the sun. My life was so restful at that time it was quite easy to cope with life without having to resort to cigarettes. So my advice to prospective quitters is keep on trying. You'll get there in the end ... if you really want to!"

Appendix

Round To It List

The Smoker's Quit Chart

Useful Addresses

THE 'ROUND TO IT' LIST

This is a list of jobs which need to be done. I will start one of these jobs whenever I feel the desire to smoke coming upon me. I must keep myself busy and occupied, as cravings do not last for long. These jobs can be done in any order.

JOB	DONE
1.	
2.	
3.	
4.	
5.	
6.	
7.	
8.	
9.	
10.	
11.	
12.	

THE SMOKER'S QUIT CHART

NAME:									Year: 19		
Jan	Feb	Mar	Apr	May	Jun	Jul	Aug	Sep	Oct	Nov	Dec
1											
2											
3											
4											
5											
6											
7											
8											
9											
10											
11											
12											
13											
14											
15											
16											
17											
18											
19											
20											
21											
22											
23											
24											
25											
26											
27											
28											
29											
30											
31											

QUIT DAY   − MARK IN RED 'Q-Day'

SMOKEFREE DAY   − ✔

IF YOU'VE SMOKED − X   Plus number of cigarettes smoked − (2)

Useful Addresses

Swift Publishers can provide you, or, in the case of employers, your firm, with further information, important addresses, audio tapes by Dr Chris Steele, information on Chris Steele's SMOKEQUITTERS STOP SMOKING PROGRAMME IN THE WORKFORCE, and other aids and materials for quitters.

If you would like more details of Swift's services for smokers and ex-smokers, please send a stamped addressed envelope to the following address:

Swift Publishers
Refuge Assurance House
Market Street
Bromsgrove
Worcestershire B61 8DA

or call us at 0527 76150 (40 lines).

DR CHRIS STEELE'S TAPE QUITLINE NUMBER

Dr Chris Steele has recorded a tape to help people stop smoking. To hear this, you need to ring the following number

0891 101223

Please note that calls are charged at 36p per minute, cheap rate, 48p per minute at other times.

OTHER USEFUL ADDRESSES

The following are charitable organisations which can provide you with anti-smoking advice free of charge:

ASH Action on Smoking and Health
109 Gloucester Place
London W1H 3PH
Tel: 071 935 3519

QUIT
102 Gloucester Place
London W1H 3DA
Tel: 071 487 2858

Health Education Authority
Hamilton House
Mabledon Place
London WC1H 9TX
Tel: 071 383 3833

NICOTINE REDUCTION THERAPY MANUFACTURERS

All of these will provide information on their nicotine replacement therapies:

Nicabate Patch

>   Marion Merrell Dow
>   Lakeside House
>   Stockley Park
>   Uxbridge
>   Middlesex UB11 1BE
>
>   Tel: 081 848 3456

Nicotinell Patch

>   Ciba-Geigy Pharmaceuticals
>   Wimblehurst Road
>   Horsham
>   West Sussex
>   RH12 4AB
>
>   SMOKEFREE HELPLINE:
>   Tel (freephone): 0800 515514

Nicorette Gum and *Nicorette* Patch

> Kabi Pharmacia
> Therapeutics Division
> Energy Park
> Davy Avenue
> Knowlhill
> Milton Keynes
> Bucks MK5 8PH
>
> NICORETTE HELP-DESK:
> Tel (freephone): 0500 390114

Niconil Patch

> Elan Pharma
> Parke-Davis Research Laboratories
> Lambert Court
> Chestnut Avenue
> Eastleigh
> Hants SO5 3ZQ
>
> Tel: 0703 620500

YOUR OPPORTUNITY TO PURCHASE ONE OF THE MOST EXCITING
AND MOVING HUMAN INTEREST STORIES OF THE CENTURY.

If you would like to purchase a copy of this book, signed by the author, please forward a cheque or postal order for £15.99 (inclusive of postage & packing) made payable to Swift Publishers Ltd at the following address:

Swift Publishers
Refuge Assurance House
Market Street
Bromsgrove
Worcestershire B61 8DA
Tel: 0527 76150 (40 lines)